SUPER POPS

60 QUICK AND TASTY CAKE POPS, COOKIE POPS, MERINGUE POPS, TOFFEE POPS & MORE

TAMSIN ASTON *WITH* JUDITH FERTIG

A QUINTET BOOK
First edition for the United States and Canada
published in 2012 by Barron's Educational
Series, Inc.

All inquiries should be addressed to:
Barron's Educational Series, Inc.
250 Wireless Boulevard
Hauppauge, NY 11788
www.barronseduc.com

Library of Congress Control Number:
2011943027
ISBN: 978-0-7641-6557-3

QTT.CCAK
Conceived, designed, and produced by
Quintet Publishing Limited
The Old Brewery
6 Blundell Street
London N7 9BH
UK

Project Editor: Chloe Todd Fordham
Consultant and Copyeditor: Cary Hull
Art Editor and Designer: Zoë White
Art Director: Michael Charles
Photographer: Simon Pask
Set Designer: Laura Phillips
Editorial Director: Donna Gregory
Publisher: Mark Searle

Printed by Shanghai Offset Printing Products Ltd,
China
9 8 7 6 5 4 3 2 1

Super POPS

Contents

Pick a Pop

Browse the selection for a cute-looking pop and turn to the relevant page to start decorating.

QUARTERBACK'S GAME
BALL, PAGE 38
TENNIS BALL, PAGE 40
SOCCER BALL, PAGE 41

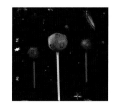

SILVER MOON, PAGE 43

BEACH BALL, PAGE 44

FRIENDLY GHOST, PAGE 47
ZOMBIE EYEBALL, PAGE 48
SPIDER WEB, PAGE 49

SIR CHOC-A-LOT, PAGE 50

DERBY WINNER, PAGE 53

ROBOT, PAGE 54

DINOSAUR, PAGE 57

DINOSAUR EGG, PAGE 58

WICKED WITCH, PAGE 61

MUG OF HOT CHOCOLATE,
PAGE 62

BABY'S RATTLE, PAGE 64
BABY DOLL, PAGE 66
RUBBER DUCKY, PAGE 67

LAVENDER HEART, PAGE 68
HEARTTHROB, PAGE 70
WINGED HEART, PAGE 71

SNOWMAN, PAGE 72
ARCTIC EXPLORER, PAGE 74
CHRISTMAS PUDDING,
PAGE 75

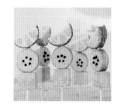

FRUIT KEBABS, PAGE 77

BABY BLOCKS, PAGE 78

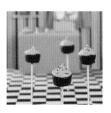

CUPCAKES, PAGE 81

AHOY, MATE!, PAGE 82
TUGBOAT, PAGE 84
DEEP SEA DIVER, PAGE 85

MOUSE, PAGE 87

PINK PIGLET, PAGE 88
CUTE COW, PAGE 90

UNNY BUNNY, PAGE 91
HEEP, PAGE 92

GNOMES, PAGE 95

WEDDING CAKE, PAGE 96

SAND CASTLE, PAGE 99

SPRING TULIP, PAGE 100

WIZARD WAND, PAGE 103

SWEET BLOSSOM,
PAGE 104

CHRISTMAS TREE,
PAGE 107

WEDDING BELLS,
PAGE 108

CLOWN, PAGE 111

  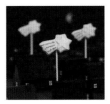  

CHESHIRE CAT, PAGE 113

BEE BLOSSOM, PAGE 114
EGG'S NEST, PAGE 116
WOODLAND MUSHROOM,
PAGE 117

SHOOTING STAR, PAGE 119

TICK TOCK, PAGE 120

SHIP'S WHEEL, PAGE 122

ST. LUCIA CANDLE,
PAGE 125

STARFISH, PAGE 126

VENETIAN MASK,
PAGE 129

SURF'S UP, PAGE 130

TORTOISE, PAGE 133

GROOVY RECORD,
PAGE 135

UFO, PAGE 136
ALIEN, PAGE 138
RINGS OF SATURN,
PAGE 139

BITTEN COOKIE, PAGE 141

Introduction

This book gives you the most colorful, whimsical, miniature confections possible. These two-bite treats-on-a-stick have shaken loose traditional cakes, cupcakes, brownies, and candies from their pans and molds and taken them into the realm of the fantastic.

We get the little ball rolling with the familiar cake pop. From there, we venture into eight more yummy concoctions that offer lots of different textures—from soft to crunchy, chewy to crackly. Dip and swirl a brownie pop in melted chocolate, then sprinkle on more chocolate, and you've got a chocoholic's dream in miniature. Bake cookie dough into cookie pop molds and create a colorful cookie pop bouquet to celebrate a friend's good news. Make a medieval army of knights-on-sticks for your chess club. Serve ghostly meringue pops at Halloween parties and beach ball pops for a weekend getaway. Whether you're an absolute beginner or a practiced dessert maker, you can find flavors, techniques, and designs that will tempt you throughout the book. One thing is certain: making pops will bring out both the kitchen wizard and the artist in you. And that's the really *super* thing about *Super Pops*. This book is a primer, a handbook, and a springboard for your own creativity—all rolled into one.

How to Use This Book

This book contains ten easy base recipes and suggested variations. These base recipes are at the heart of the pop projects in the final chapter, and you will need to refer back to the base recipes section (pages 19–29) often when designing and decorating your pops. Each base recipe has been given a colored icon, as depicted above, which will appear throughout the book for easy reference. The base recipes indicated in the project section are recommendations only. When you have made your pop with the recommended base recipe, try one of the variations, or even a different base altogether. The times given in Chapter 4 denote decorating time for one pop only, assuming the chocolate has been melted, the royal icing colored and in the piping bag ready for piping, and the fondant tinted.

Super POPS

Chapter 1

Getting Started

Equipment

The recipes in this book require only the most basic kitchen equipment.

Mixers and Mixing Bowls (1)

A handheld or a stand mixer with a whisk attachment are must-haves for meringues and marshmallows, which require vigorous beating of the egg whites. Electric mixers are helpful in making marshmallow pops, allowing you to pour in the hot syrup more easily, while beating the whites. Stainless steel bowls are ideal, as they chill fast for making truffles and don't stain when you're tinting fondant or gum paste.

Rolling Pin (2)

A sturdy rolling pin is necessary for rolling out cookie dough for cookie pops as well as fondant and gum paste for decorations.

Selection of Dessert-Making Tools

Base mixtures for pops entail regular dessert-making tools. For example, spatulas (4) transfer meringue to a piping bag or cake and brownie batters to their pans. Truffle pops come together best with a whisk (14), after you've poured the hot cream over the chocolate in a mixing bowl. A small cookie scoop or melon baller (7) is used to scoop a chilled base mixture into balls. Table or paring knives (3) cut some pop mixtures into basic shapes or help nudge candy pops out of their molds.

Kitchen Scissors (5)

You'll need sharp and sturdy kitchen scissors to cut sugar sheets, stick gum, or shoelace candy.

Piping Bag and Tips (6)

With a piping bag and an assortment of large and small tips, you can pipe meringue pops into shapes or add decorative details to other types of pops. You can buy a reusable piping bag and an assortment of tips, which are applicable to many other uses, or you can simply buy disposable plastic piping bags and tips just for pops.

Cookie Cutters (8)

Sturdy cookie cutters allow you to cut out shapes for a variety of pops. Select simple cookie cutter shapes without a lot of fine details, so the pop base mixture releases more easily.

Lollipop sticks (9)

The rounded paper lollipop stick holds well in all kinds of mixtures.

Saucepans (10)
Homemade candy pop bases cook in a matter of minutes in a saucepan on the stove top. Although you can make a candy mixture in almost any saucepan, heavy-bottomed pans resist scorching more easily. For melting candy coating wafers or chocolate, use a double boiler or bain-marie.

Fondant Modeling Tools (11)
Fondant modeling tools are available in stores, and are useful for molding and manipulating fondant and gum pastes.

Edible pen (12)
Edible pens (sold at cake decorating supply stores) that can write on chocolate are ideal for adding details to pops.

Watercolor Paintbrush (13)
A clean paintbrush is useful for painting fine details on pops.

Measuring Cups and Spoons (15)
Measuring accurately is essential for the success of these pops. Use calibrated measuring cups and spoons. When measuring flour, scoop it from the bag or canister, then pour it into the measuring cup, and level it off.

Candy Thermometer (16)
When you're making candy, you measure the temperature of the sugar mixture with a candy thermometer, which lets you know at a glance when the mixture has reached the proper point in a recipe.

Pop Molds (17)
Uniquely shaped pop molds, made from metal or silicone, help form individual pops, with a special place to insert the lollipop stick. Unless you own several molds, you will need to make some recipes in batches.

Baking Pans and Baking Sheets
Cake, cookie, and brownie pops call for baking pans—cake and mini-muffin pans and baking sheets.

Styrofoam
A block of Styrofoam gives you a handy place to insert pops-in-progress so they can cool and/or dry.

Ingredients

There are so many decorating ingredients to select from. Here are some pop favorites.

Sugar Sheets or Rice Paper (1)

Cake decorators and pop makers use sugar sheets, which are flat, rectangular pieces of worked sugar, about the size of computer paper. Sugar sheets are similar in texture to stick chewing gum and come in a variety of patterns from stripes to small prints. Sold at cake decorating stores, they're perfect for making flat, precise, decorative shapes like bands or circles or borders. You can easily cut sugar sheets into shapes with kitchen scissors or a sharp paring knife or use a special sugar sheet cutter for more intricate work.

Colored Sugar (3)

Buy colored sugar in cake decorating stores, or make your own by adding a speck of food coloring with a toothpick to your sugar and mixing well. Rolling your pops in colored sugar gives them a lovely texture and a little sparkle.

Fondant (5)

Fondant is a sturdy, smooth icing that can be tinted and rolled. Wedding cake decorators have long used fondant to add a sleek finish to cakes. Fondant can be rolled to many different sizes, from the smallest decorative detail to covering a large cake layer. Like modeling clay, but edible, fondant can also be hand-molded

into many different, somewhat flat pop details. Most cake decorating and craft stores sell packaged white fondant that you can tint and/or roll at home. Some stores also sell ready-made rolled fondant as well as ready-made colored fondants.

Gum paste (6)

Gum paste is a more granular cake-decorating product that is used mainly for making decorative details like roses and other flowers for wedding cakes. Gum paste is a firmer mixture than fondant. Although it can also be tinted, hand-molded, and rolled, gum paste is not as smooth, soft, or malleable as

fondant. Gum paste holds its shape for three-dimensional details much better than fondant or sugar sheets, but it can dry out quickly. If you want to make gum paste decorations ahead of time, store them in an airtight container so they don't dry out.

Coating Wafers (7)
Also known as candy melts, these wafers are made of sweetened white chocolate, which is already tinted and sometimes flavored.

Food Coloring (11)
Food coloring liquids or gels adds color to base mixtures, fondant, gum paste, and icings.

Edible Glue (12)
Just as it sounds, this cake decorator's product helps decorations adhere to any kind of pop. You can also use a little dab of melted candy coating wafers or chocolate.

Cake Decorations and Candies
Cake decorations such as colored or chocolate sprinkles, colored sugars, sanding sugars that look like flattened crystals, popping candy/space dust (9), sugar pearls (14), edible glitter (10), or chocolate-coated cookie sticks (2) can be used in many recipes. More intricate pops might also use ready-made decorations such as gum paste hearts (8), marshmallows (4),

shoelace candy and button candy, as well as hard candies like LifeSavers. Feel free to use your imagination and creativity by dreaming up other ways to use ready-made sweets to decorate your pops.

White and Dark Chocolate (13)
The best-tasting pops come from the best-tasting chocolate, especially in truffle pops. When in doubt, go for the better brand rather than the bargain offering.

Showing Off Your Pops

Once you've crafted your signature pops, you'll want to display them for maximum effect. Depending on a pop's design, it can either be showcased standing up with support, as from a Styrofoam block, or upside down on a plate or platter.

Deciding on a Support System

At craft and hobby shops, you can buy white Styrofoam in many different shapes and sizes, including blocks, hearts, stars, cones, balls, sheets, poles, discs, crosses, and wreaths or rings. Using an electric, serrated, or craft knife, you can also cut the Styrofoam into a desired shape or to fit inside baskets or any other type of container. You can cover the Styrofoam with decorative papers, craft grass, ribbon, artificial flowers, edible gold coins, or other thematic material. Use a white craft glue to make sure the decorations adhere. Then, let the Styrofoam dry for at least 15 minutes before displaying the pops upright.

You can also show off your pops in special clear acrylic or white plastic pop holders (shown right), which are available at craft and baking supply stores. Or make a paper dollie, create a hole in the middle, and push the pop's lollipop stick through to create a pretty presentation base. Another option is to put the pops into little cellophane bags and tie with a twist tie or a ribbon. They will look pretty and the cellophane will keep the pops fresh. Add ribbons tied into a bow around the lollipop sticks, or to make the pops personal, add cardboard name tags.

Deciding on a Design

Once you have decided on your support system, you can take the pop design further. Start with the theme of your pop and go from there. For example, create a gray stone castle out of Styrofoam blocks, cones, and rings so your Sir Choc-a-Lot Cake Pops (page 50) can guard it or would-be wizards can practice with Honeycomb Wizard Wand Pops (page 103). Cover a block with artificial snow, then invite a convention of Snowman Marshmallow Pops (page 72) to gather. Place Styrofoam in a basket and cover it with craft grass so floral-themed pops such as Bee Blossom Cookie Pops (page 114) or Spring Tulip Brownie Pops (page 100) can bloom. Create your own universe with a half-dome Styrofoam

studded with Shooting Star Cookie Pops (page 119) or UFO Chewy Toffee Pops (page 136). Arrange your Woodland Mushroom Meringue Pops (page 117) on a Styrofoam "log." Always arrange your pops in the Styrofoam block so that the large pops do not obscure the smaller pops and so that the colors complement each other.

Displaying Non-Vertical Pops

Other Super Pops can lie down on the display job. Simply served on white plate or platter, pops like Soccer Ball (page 41) make a grab-and-go treat perfect for children's parties. If you want to get fancy, sprinkle a plate or platter with a coordinating colored sugar, pearls, or sprinkles, and simply serve pops like Baby Blocks Marshmallow Pops (page 78) upside down.

Super POPS

Chilling 1½ hours · Yellow Cake · makes 17-20

Yellow Cake

Combine cake crumbs with a cream cheese frosting to make a delicious mixture—and it's so easy to mold into cake pops! This yellow cake base is great for pops that will be dipped in lighter colors of melted candy coating, because the cake doesn't show through the coating.

INGREDIENTS

For the cake:
- ½ cup (1 stick) unsalted butter, softened
- ½ cup plus 1 tbsp. granulated sugar
- 1 tsp. vanilla extract
- 2 large eggs
- 1 cup all-purpose flour
- 1 tsp. baking powder
- ¼ tsp. salt

For the frosting:
- 1⅓ cups confectioners' sugar
- 6 tbsp. unsalted butter, softened
- 2 oz. cream cheese
- 1 tsp. vanilla extract

Making the Cake

Preheat the oven to 350°F (175°C) and line a 9-inch (23-cm) cake pan with waxed paper. In the bowl of an electric mixer, cream the butter and sugar together until light and fluffy. Beat in the vanilla, then the eggs, one at a time. Sift the dry ingredients into a small bowl, then add to the batter. Mix until smoothly blended. Spoon the thick batter into the prepared pan and smooth the top. Bake for 25–27 minutes or until a toothpick inserted in the center comes out clean. Transfer to a wire rack to cool in the pan. The cake can be made up to 3 days ahead, covered with plastic wrap, and stored on the kitchen counter.

Making the Frosting

Mix all ingredients together until smooth and thick. Cover and refrigerate, unless you're using it soon. The frosting can be made 2 days ahead and kept covered in the refrigerator. Let sit at room temperature for 30 minutes before using.

Making the Pop Base

To make the yellow cake pop base, crumble the cooled cake into fine crumbs into a large bowl or the bowl of a food processor. Add the frosting and blend by hand or pulse in the food processor until the mixture forms a mass and you can pinch off a piece and roll it into a ball without cracking. If necessary, add a few drops of water to the cake pop base to moisten. Cover with plastic wrap and refrigerate for at least 1 hour (or up to 3 days) before using.

NOW TRY THIS

PRINCESS CAKE
For the frosting, use 1 teaspoon almond extract in addition to the vanilla extract. Proceed with the recipe.

ORANGE CAKE
For the frosting, add 2 teaspoons grated orange zest in addition to the vanilla extract. Proceed with the recipe.

LEMON CAKE
For the cake, add 2 teaspoons grated lemon zest with the eggs. Proceed with the recipe.

STORING THE POPS
Pre-dipped pops can be frozen. Thaw out before dipping. Once decorated, yellow cake pops can be stored in an airtight container in the refrigerator for up to 1 week.

Making: 2 hours · Chilling: 1½ hours · Chocolate Cake · makes 22-26

Chocolate Cake

Chocolate cake crumbs and chocolate frosting combine for a lovely, chocolaty moldable mixture for cake pops. This chocolate cake pop base works well for pops that will be dipped in darker colors of melted candy coating, so the cake won't show through.

INGREDIENTS

For the cake:

3 tbsp. unsweetened cocoa powder

½ cup boiling water

½ cup (1 stick) unsalted butter, softened

1 cup granulated sugar

1 tsp. vanilla extract

2 large eggs

1¼ cups all-purpose flour

1¼ tsp. baking powder

¼ tsp. baking soda

½ tsp. salt

For the frosting:

1⅓ cups confectioners' sugar

½ cup (1 stick) unsalted butter, softened

⅔ cup semisweet chocolate chips, melted and cooled

1 tbsp. whole milk

Making the Cake

Preheat the oven to 350°F and line a 9-inch (23-cm) cake pan with waxed paper. Combine the cocoa powder and boiling water in a small bowl. Set aside to cool slightly. In the bowl of an electric mixer, cream the butter and sugar together until light and fluffy. Beat in the vanilla, then the eggs, one at a time. Sift the dry ingredients into a small bowl, then add to the batter. Mix until just blended. Stir in the cooled cocoa mixture until the batter is uniformly brown. Spoon the thick batter into the prepared pan and smooth the top. Bake for 33–35 minutes or until a toothpick inserted in the center comes out clean. Transfer to a wire rack to cool in the pan. The cake can be made up to 3 days ahead, covered with plastic wrap, and stored on the kitchen counter.

Making the Frosting

Mix all ingredients together until smooth and thick. Cover and refrigerate, unless you're using it soon. The frosting can be made 2 days ahead and kept covered in the refrigerator. Let sit at room temperature for 30 minutes before using.

Making the Pop Base

Crumble the cooled cake into fine crumbs into a bowl or the bowl of a food processor. Add the frosting and blend by hand or pulse in the food processor until the mixture forms a mass and you can pinch off a piece and roll it into a ball without cracking. If necessary, add a few drops of water to moisten. Cover with plastic wrap and refrigerate for at least 1 hour (or up to 3 days) before using.

NOW TRY THIS

COCONUT CHOCOLATE CAKE
In the frosting recipe, use ⅓ cup coconut milk in place of the softened butter and proceed with the recipe.

MEXICAN CHOCOLATE CAKE
In the frosting recipe, use chopped Mexican chocolate (available in the Hispanic section at grocery stores) in place of chocolate chips.

RED VELVET CAKE
In the cake recipe, use ⅓ cup boiling water in place of ½ cup water and stir in 1 (1.5-oz.) bottle of red food coloring. Proceed with the recipe.

STORING THE POPS
Pre-dipped pops can be frozen. Thaw out before dipping. Once decorated, chocolate cake pops can be stored in an airtight container in the refrigerator for up to 2 weeks.

Chilling 2-4 hours   Meringue   makes 24-36

Meringue

Whipping up clouds of meringue can inspire a bit of whimsy.

INGREDIENTS

4 egg whites, at room temperature
½ tsp. cream of tartar
1½ cups confectioners' sugar
1 tsp. vanilla extract

Making the Pop Base

In a glass or metal mixing bowl, with an electric mixer, beat the egg whites until frothy on a medium speed. Add the cream of tartar and increase the speed to high until soft peaks form. Still whisking, slowly add the sugar, a tablespoonful at a time. Wait 20 seconds between each addition to make sure the sugar has dissolved and the whites are stiff and glossy and forming stiff peaks. (A test to check this is to rub a small amount between your fingers; it should not feel gritty.) Whisk in the vanilla extract for 30 seconds. Use immediately in one of the meringue pop recipes.

TIPS

• To make sure your meringue pops keep their shapes and don't soften, make them during dry—not humid—weather.
• Make sure the egg whites are at room temperature and not straight from the refrigerator, as they will more quickly whisk higher and lighter.
• If you have used your mixing bowl and beaters for batters that contain butter or oil, pour a drop of distilled vinegar in the bowl and wipe it and the beaters dry with a paper towel before starting this recipe. Just a little bit of fat can deflate the meringue.

NOW TRY THIS

MOCHA MERINGUE
In place of ¼ cup of the confectioners' sugar, add 2 teaspoons instant coffee powder. Proceed with the recipe.

CRUSHED CANDY MERINGUE
Carefully fold ½ cup finely crushed hard candies (or to taste) into the prepared meringue.

TINTED MERINGUE
Add drops of food coloring in the desired shade before adding the sugar, then proceed with the recipe.

STORING THE POPS
Store in an airtight container for up to 1 week.

22

Honeycomb

Sometimes known as seafoam candy because of the bubbles inside, this traditional sweet is easy to make.

INGREDIENTS
4 tbsp. unsalted butter
¾ cup plus 1 tbsp. granulated sugar
¼ cup light corn syrup
2 tsp. baking soda

Making the Pop Base
Have the oiled molds ready before preparing honeycomb candy. In a saucepan over a low heat, stir the butter, sugar, and corn syrup together until the butter has melted and the sugar has dissolved. Raise the heat to medium-high and bring the mixture to a boil. Cook for about 5 minutes, or until the mixture turns into a golden brown syrup (you can check with a candy thermometer; it should read 150°F (65°C)). Remove the saucepan from the heat and whisk in the baking soda with a fork for a few seconds until the mixture bubbles up. Use right away in one of the honeycomb pop recipes.

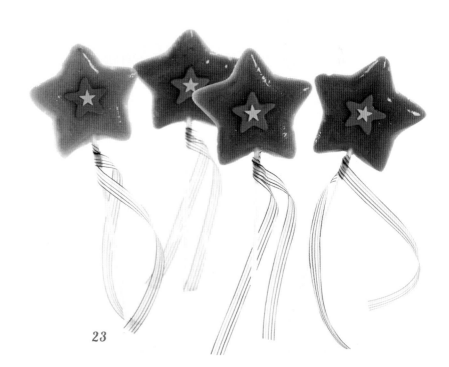

23

Chilling 1 hour · *makes 10-20*

Truffle

Smooth, delicious chocolate truffles create the base for small, oh-so-delicious treats. You can easily flavor them with white chocolate, powdered espresso or coffee, rum, chocolate-hazelnut spread, or vanilla.

INGREDIENTS

- 6 oz. semisweet or dark chocolate chips or pieces (about 1 cup)
- ½ cup heavy or whipping cream
- 2 tbsp. (1 oz.) unsalted butter, softened
- 1 tsp. vanilla extract

Making the Pop Base

Heat the chocolate and cream in a bowl over a saucepan of simmering water until the chocolate has melted. Whisk in the butter, then whisk in the vanilla extract. Refrigerate for at least 1 hour or until very, very cold.

TIPS

The trick to forming the truffle shapes—without getting your hands too messy—is getting the truffle mixture really, really cold and working quickly in a cool kitchen.

WHITE CHOCOLATE AND RUM TRUFFLE
Instead of the base recipe, use 5½ ounces white chocolate chips, 3 tablespoons cream, 5 tablespoons butter, and 1 teaspoon rum extract.

ESPRESSO BEAN TRUFFLE
Whisk 2 teaspoons instant espresso (or your favorite coffee powder) into the hot cream and chocolate. Proceed with the recipe.

HAZELNUT AND DARK CHOCOLATE TRUFFLE
Substitute 2 tablespoons (1 oz.) chocolate-hazelnut spread for the butter. Proceed with the recipe.

STORING THE POPS
Keep in an airtight container in the refrigerator for up to 3 days. Take them out 30 minutes before eating to let them come to room temperature. Truffles can be frozen before dipping and decorating, but remember to thaw out before dipping.

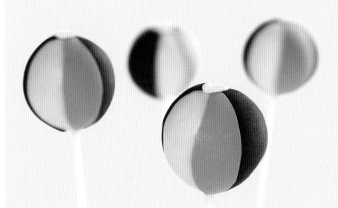

Making 95 mins — Setting 6 hours — Marsh Mallow — *makes* 12-24

Marshmallow

**Homemade marshmallows are a revelation! So ooey, gooey, and fun.
And so easy to make.**

INGREDIENTS

1 tbsp. cornstarch
1 tbsp. confectioners' sugar
Vegetable oil

For the syrup:
2½ cups granulated sugar
¼ tsp. salt
1⅛ cups water

For the gelatin mixture:
1 oz. unflavored gelatin
  powder
½ cup boiling water
1 tsp. vanilla extract
2 egg whites

Before you Begin

Decide which marshmallow pop recipe you will be making
—one prepared in individual molds or a recipe in which the
marshmallow is cut into shapes after it has become firm in
baking dishes.

For individual molds: In a bowl, mix together the
cornstarch and confectioners' sugar. Brush silicone molds
with vegetable oil. Dust the molds with the cornstarch and
sugar mixture.

For a baking dish: In a bowl, mix together the cornstarch and
confectioners' sugar. Oil a 9 x 13-inch (22 x 33-cm) glass baking
dish or two 8-inch (20-cm) square silicone baking dishes. If using
the glass dish, line it with baking parchment, allowing a 2-inch
(5-cm) overhang on the long sides, and brush the parchment
paper with oil. Dust the dish with the cornstarch and sugar
mixture. (It is important to use the correct size dish because the
marshmallow is cut into shapes directly from the dish.)

Making the Syrup

To make the syrup, stir the granulated sugar, salt, and water
together in a medium saucepan. Bring to a boil over low heat,
while stirring to dissolve the sugar. Turn up the heat to high
and boil without stirring, until the syrup registers 250°F (122°C)
(hard ball stage) on a candy thermometer, about 8–9 minutes.

Making the Pop Base

Add the gelatin to the boiling water. Stir until it has dissolved
and then add to the hot syrup. Meanwhile, beat 2 egg whites
until they are quite stiff. On low speed, whisk the hot syrup into
the egg whites. Gradually increase the speed to high. Keep beating
until the mixture is very stiff and white, about 12 minutes. Beat
in the vanilla. Pour the marshmallow into the prepared dish or
molds, and smooth with an offset spatula. Set aside, uncovered,
for about 6 hours or until firm.

NOW TRY THIS

COCONUT MARSHMALLOW
In place of the
vanilla extract, use
coconut extract.
Proceed with the recipe.

CINNAMON SPICE MARSHMALLOW
In place of the vanilla, use 2
teaspoons ground cinnamon
and 1 teaspoon ground allspice.
Proceed with the recipe.

ROMANTIC ROSE MARSHMALLOW
In place of 1 teaspoon vanilla
extract, use 1 teaspoon vanilla
and 1 teaspoon rosewater. Tint
the marshmallow pink with red
food coloring before spreading
it in the dish.

CITRUS MARSHMALLOW
In place of vanilla, use 2
teaspoons lemon or orange
extract and 1 teaspoon
powdered citric acid (available
in the canning or kosher section
of supermarkets). Tint the
marshmallow with yellow food
coloring before spreading it in
the dish.

STORING THE POPS
If the pop has fondant
decorations, eat them on the
same day; otherwise, store in
an airtight container for up to
1 week.

Chilling 1 hour · Cookie · makes 24-30

Cookie

Everyone loves sugar cookies, and this recipe makes a sweet dough that is easy to roll out. For cookie pops, you'll roll the dough out to a ¼-inch (6-mm) thickness or more so that the cookies keep their shapes better.

INGREDIENTS

For the cookie:
¾ cup (12 tablespoons) unsalted butter, softened
1 cup granulated sugar
2 large eggs
1 teaspoon vanilla extract
1½ cups all-purpose flour, plus more for rolling out
1 teaspoon baking powder
¾ teaspoon salt

For the frosting:
2 egg whites
4 cups confectioners' sugar
1 tsp. vanilla extract
Water or milk for thinning
Food coloring (optional)

Making the Pop Base

In a large bowl, cream together the butter and sugar until light and fluffy. Beat in the eggs and vanilla. Stir in the flour, baking powder, and salt until you have a smooth dough. Cover and chill the dough for at least 1 hour or overnight before rolling out.

Making the Frosting

Whisk the egg whites until frothy, then slowly add the confectioners' sugar while whisking. Add vanilla and enough water or milk to make a solid yet pourable consistency. Tint the frosting with food coloring, if desired.

NOW TRY THIS

SUGAR 'N' SPICE COOKIE
Omit the vanilla extract and add 1 teaspoon ground ginger and 1 teaspoon cinnamon to the dry ingredients. Proceed with the recipe.

ALMOND SPRITZ COOKIE
In place of vanilla, use 1 teaspoon almond extract and proceed with the recipe.

FRESH LIME COOKIE
In place of vanilla, use the grated zest of 1 lime and proceed with the recipe.

SWEDISH CARDAMOM COOKIE
In addition to vanilla, add ½ teaspoon ground cardamom and proceed with the recipe.

STORING THE POPS
Once dry, store cookie pops in an airtight container in a cool place (not the refrigerator) and eat within 1–2 weeks.

Making 40 mins · Chilling 1/2 hour · Brownie · *makes 16-20*

Brownie

These moist chocolaty brownies are easy to make. You'll use brownie pop pans (or mini-muffin pans) for the pop recipes.

INGREDIENTS

3 large eggs
⅔ cup granulated sugar
½ cup light brown sugar
1 tsp. vanilla extract
10 tbsp. (5 oz.) unsalted
    butter, melted
1 cup cocoa powder
½ cup all-purpose flour
½ tsp. salt

Making the Pop Base

Preheat oven. In a medium mixing bowl, beat the eggs and the sugars together until well combined, smooth, and glossy. Beat in the vanilla and the melted butter. Sift together the cocoa powder, flour, and salt into a bowl. Fold the dry ingredients into the egg mixture. Pour the mixture into the pop molds. Bake in a 350°F (175°C) oven for 25-30 minutes. The brownies are ready when a toothpick comes out clean when inserted into the center.

TIPS

Remember to fill each brownie pop mold only two-thirds full of batter. Each mold will make 8 brownie pops in the shape of large gumdrops. Brownies are done when they start to pull away from the sides of the mold.

NOW TRY THIS

CHOCOLATE MINT BROWNIE
In place of vanilla, use peppermint extract and proceed with the recipe.

DOUBLE CHOCOLATE BROWNIE
After filling each mold, press 3 chocolate chips into each one, and proceed with the recipe.

ROCKY ROAD BROWNIE
Place 3 miniature marshmallows in each prepared mold, then fill ⅔ full with batter. Proceed with the recipe.

STORING THE POPS
Brownies can be made ahead and frozen before being dipped and decorated. Thaw out before dipping. Brownie pops will keep in the refrigerator for up to 5 days in an airtight container.

Butter Brittle

This light brown caramel candy has just enough butter to crunch and crack when you take a bite. Have your pans ready before starting to make the Butter Brittle, because once it's ready to pour into molds it needs to be used immediately.

INGREDIENTS

2 tbsp. water
½ cup (1 stick) salted or unsalted butter, cut into pieces
¼ tsp. salt
1 cup granulated sugar
¼ cup packed light brown sugar
¼ tsp. baking soda
1 tsp. vanilla extract

Making the Pop Base

In a medium saucepan fitted with a candy thermometer, heat the water, butter, salt, granulated sugar, and light brown sugar over low heat until the sugars have melted. Increase the temperature to medium–high. Cook, stirring as little as possible, until the thermometer reads 300°F (150°C) and the mixture has turned a light brown, about 12 minutes. Remove from the heat and immediately stir in the baking soda and vanilla. Use immediately.

NOW TRY THIS

BUTTER BRITTLE WITH ALMONDS

Divide 1 cup toasted and finely chopped blanched almonds among the prepared molds before inserting the lollipop stick and pouring in the just-made brittle.

BUTTER BRITTLE WITH PEANUTS

Divide 1 cup whole, roasted red-skinned Spanish peanuts among the prepared molds before inserting the lollipop stick and pouring in the just-made brittle.

STORING THE POPS
Store in an airtight container in a cool place, with parchment paper separating the pops. Will keep for 2 weeks.

Chewy Toffee

These easy caramels cool to a soft, chewy texture. Prepare your pans before starting to make the toffee base because once it's ready to pour into molds it needs to be used immediately.

INGREDIENTS

½ cup (1 stick) unsalted butter, cut into pieces
1 cup granulated sugar
1 cup firmly packed light brown sugar
½ cup whole milk
½ cup heavy or whipping cream
½ cup light corn syrup
½ tsp. salt
1 tsp. vanilla extract

Making the Pop Base

In a medium saucepan fitted with a candy thermometer, heat the butter, granulated and light brown sugars, milk, cream, corn syrup, and salt over low heat until the sugars have melted. Increase the temperature to medium–high and bring to a boil. Cook, stirring as little as possible, until the thermometer reads 300°F (150°C) and the mixture has turned medium brown, about 18–20 minutes. Remove from the heat and stir in the vanilla. Use immediately.

NOW TRY THIS

CHEWY ORANGE TOFFEE
In place of vanilla, add 2 teaspoons freshly grated orange zest.

CHEWY LAVENDER TOFFEE
With the vanilla, add 1 teaspoon very finely chopped dried, organic lavender buds.

STORING THE POPS
Store in an airtight container in a cool place, with parchment paper separating the pops. Will keep for 2 weeks.

Super
POPS

Chapter 3
Decorating

Securing the Lollipop Sticks

All of the recipes in Super Pops call for paper lollipop sticks. When and where you insert them depends on the type of pop you're making.

Cake Pops

Dip the tip of a lollipop stick into melted chocolate or candy coating wafers and simply insert it into the base of a cake pop. Place each pop, stick up, on a prepared baking sheet. Set aside for 15 minutes at room temperature. The stick should be firmly attached to the pop in about 15 minutes.

Truffle Pops

To secure the stick in a truffle pop, insert the tip of a stick into the base of a truffle pop, then swirl the whole pop in melted candy coating wafers or melted chocolate. Set it in a block of Styrofoam to dry.

Marshmallow Pops

Because the marshmallow mixture is so sticky, lollipop sticks usually have no trouble adhering. But if necessary, you can always dip the stick in melted candy coating wafers, melted chocolate, or edible glue.

Cookie Pops

Cookie pop molds have a place for the lollipop stick to go. You simply press the dough on top of the stick in the mold before baking. For cut-out cookies, you can attach the stick to the back of the cookie with melted candy coating wafers, melted chocolate, or edible glue.

Meringue Pops

For meringue pops, you can simply dip a lollipop stick in melted chocolate or candy coating wafers or in edible glue, then gently insert it into the base of the pop so the meringue doesn't crack. Set the pop in a block of Styrofoam for about 15 minutes until the stick is firmly attached.

Honeycomb, Butter Brittle, and Chewy Toffee Pops

Special pop molds have a place for the lollipop stick to go. You oil the molds well, then place the lollipop sticks so that they reach to the center of each mold. When you pour in the hot candy mixture, the lollipop stick becomes secured as the candy cools. For chewy toffee pops made in well-oiled mini-muffin pans, you pour the hot toffee mixture into each muffin cup. After the toffee has cooled for 2 minutes, insert a stick straight into the center and let the toffee continue cooling so that the stick is secure.

Brownie Pops

After you pour the brownie batter into each mold, let the brownies bake for a while, then insert the sticks in the center of each brownie pop during the last few minutes of baking. The sticks will bake into the brownie pop. However, if you encounter a stick that just won't adhere, you can attach it with edible glue, melted chocolate, or candy coating wafers.

Dip the lollipop stick in melted candy coating wafer (shown here) or chocolate before inserting into the yellow cake base.

Sometimes a flat surface helps the stick to adhere. This is especially the case for brownie pops.

Coating the Pops

Coating the pops is easy when you know how. Using a low heating temperature is the key to successfully melting candy wafers and chocolate. Just follow these instructions.

Step One

For melting chocolate or candy coating wafers (shown here), you can use a double boiler, or create your own by placing a small pan or heatproof bowl of coating wafers or chocolate over a larger saucepan of barely simmering (not boiling) water.

Step Three

Once the lollipop sticks are secure (see opposite) and the candy coating or chocolate has melted, swirl the pop in the mixture. The melted coating/chocolate will stay warm for about 15 minutes, so it's best to work quickly. Simply hold the pop by its stick, turn it upside down, and dip the pop into the melted mixture. Swirl it clockwise until the pop is smoothly coated.

Step Two

Add a few teaspoons of vegetable oil (without it the candy melts will be too thick) and stir or whisk to help all the pieces to melt. Alternatively, use the microwave on the lowest or defrost setting. Do not allow any water to mix with the candy melts as they will seize up.

Step Four

Tap the sticks on the side of the mixing bowl while turning to allow the excess candy melt to drip off, and to ensure an even finish. Place the dipped and swirled pops in a block of Styrofoam to cool.

Decorating the Pops

Now it's time for the fun part: decorating your pops. The decorations can be as simple as a dusting of sprinkles or as intricate as facial expressions made with fondant or gum paste.

Fondant and Gum Paste

Some cake decorating and craft stores offer a wide variety of fondant colors, or you can tint white fondant to whatever color you wish. A good tip is to tint more than you anticipate using, as it can be difficult to achieve the same color in a second batch. Like fondant, gum paste is a malleable mixture, but with a more translucent quality.

Tinting Fondant or Gum Paste ⬇

Place the fondant or gum paste on a non-stick surface. Add just a drop or two of food coloring and work it in with your hands. (Wear food service gloves if you don't want to color your hands.) Work the fondant or gum paste as you would modeling clay until it is a uniform color throughout, to the thickness desired. Place the tinted fondant or gum paste in a sealable plastic container to keep it moist until you want to use it.

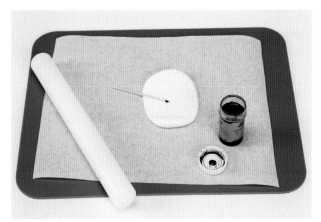

Rolling Fondant or Gum Paste ⬇

If necessary, dust the work surface and the rolling pin with a very small amount of confectioners' sugar. Roll the fondant (shown here) or gum paste with a rolling pin to the thickness desired.

Sculpting Fondant or Gum Paste ⬇

For little decorative details like tiny ears or eyes, you can simply pinch off small pieces of fondant and work them with your hands to achieve the desired detail. Attach the fondant with edible glue or melted candy coating wafers. Pinch off small pieces of gum paste to form flower petals or other details. Sturdier gum paste forms three-dimensional, yet more delicate, details better than softer, smoother, flatter fondant.

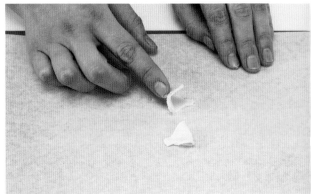

Piping Decorations with a Piping Bag

You can use a piping bag, fitted with a small tip, to pipe decorative elements onto each pop using soft mixtures like icing or melted store-bought marshmallow.

Assembling the Bag

To assemble a piping bag, you simply insert the metal or plastic tip through the large opening in the bag until the tip has come through the smaller opening in the piping bag.

Piping ⇧

To pipe, you need both hands. Holding the bag so it is horizontal, put your fingertip over the end of the tip; then, with the other hand, twist and squeeze the large end of the bag until you can feel that you've moved the piping mixture all the way to the tip and the bag is firm. Now, aim the bag with one hand and squeeze with the other to pipe details on your pop. (You will probably want to practice this before piping onto the pop.) When the detail is completed, hold the tip down, then bring it up sharply to stop piping.

Filling the Bag ⇧

To fill the bag, hold the bag with one hand and spoon the piping mixture in with the other.

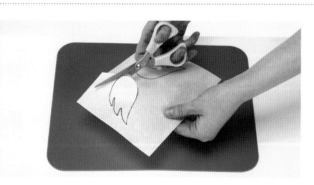

Using Sugar Sheets ⇧

Simply cut sugar sheets into shapes with scissors or a sharp knife or use a special sugar sheet cutter for more intricate work. They're perfect for making flat, precise decorative shapes like bands or circles. Like gum paste, sugar sheets dry out quickly, so use the shapes right away or store them in a plastic container.

Painting Decorations ⇧

You can use an edible pen, one that writes well on chocolate, to add details to your pops. You can also use a fine, clean, watercolor-type paintbrush to paint on melted candy coating or chocolate to create expressions, lines, dots, or other embellishments (as shown here).

Super
POPS

Chapter 4
Here Come the Pops!

5 mins · *makes* 10-20

Quarterback's Game Ball

For the forward pass that wins the game! Serve these treats when you're watching your favorite quarterback on television.

POP BASE INGREDIENTS
Chocolate Truffle Base, page 24

DECORATING INGREDIENTS
8 oz. (½ bag) brown candy coating wafers (more if necessary)
Paper lollipop sticks
4 oz. white candy coating wafers

TO MAKE THE QUARTERBACK'S GAME BALL POPS
Line a baking sheet with parchment paper. Remove the truffle mixture from the refrigerator. Scoop balls from the mixture using a small cookie scoop or large melon baller. Form into football shapes and place on the prepared pan. Place in the refrigerator for 30 minutes.

Step One
Melt the brown candy coating wafers in a bowl over simmering water or in the microwave on the defrost setting. Remove from the heat.

Step Two
Remove the truffle pops from the refrigerator and insert a lollipop stick halfway into each. Dip and swirl each pop in the warm brown candy coating. Insert each lollipop stick in a block of Styrofoam and let dry for 15 minutes.

Step Three
Melt the white candy coating wafers in a bowl over simmering water or in the microwave on the defrost setting. Remove from the heat. Use the fine paintbrush to outline the laces on each football. Set aside to dry in a cool place for 15 minutes. Will keep in an airtight container in the refrigerator for up to 3 days.

White chocolate and rum truffle tennis ball, see page 40; chocolate truffle soccer ball, see page 41

truffle 10 mins makes 10-20

Tennis Ball

Tennis was never so delicious! Bring these as a treat for after your doubles match—or give them to your favorite future Wimbledon star.

POP BASE INGREDIENTS
White Chocolate and Rum Truffle Base, page 24

DECORATING INGREDIENTS
8 oz. (½ bag) yellow candy coating wafers (more if necessary)
Paper lollipop sticks
2 oz. white candy coating wafers
Edible glue
Yellow sugar sprinkles or edible yellow glitter

TO MAKE THE TENNIS BALL POPS
Line a baking sheet with parchment paper. Remove the truffle mixture from the refrigerator. Scoop balls from the mixture using a small cookie scoop or large melon baller. Roll into smooth balls and place on the prepared pan. Refrigerate for 30 minutes.

Step One
Melt the yellow candy coating wafers in a bowl over simmering water or in the microwave on the defrost setting. Remove from the heat.

Step Two
Remove the truffle pops from the refrigerator and insert a lollipop stick halfway into each. Dip and swirl each pop in the warm yellow candy coating. Insert each lollipop stick into a block of Styrofoam and let dry for 15 minutes.

Step Three
Melt the white candy coating wafers in a bowl over simmering water or in the microwave on the defrost setting. Remove from the heat. Using a very fine, narrow paintbrush, paint white seams on each tennis ball. Set aside to dry in a cool place for 5 minutes. Then, with a clean paintbrush, brush on edible glue between and around the white lines. Sprinkle the yellow sugar or glitter over the ball. Set aside to dry for 15 minutes. Will keep in an airtight container in the refrigerator for up to 3 days.

15 mins · makes 10-20

Soccer Ball

Underneath the white candy coating of this soccer ball lurks a delicious, toothsome, dark chocolate truffle—the kind of "mud" you don't mind having.

POP BASE INGREDIENTS
Chocolate Truffle Base, page 24

DECORATING INGREDIENTS
8 oz. (½ bag) white candy coating wafers (more if necessary)
Paper lollipop sticks
4 oz. fondant, tinted black
Black decorating icing
4 oz. brown candy coating wafers

TO MAKE THE SOCCER BALL POPS
Line a baking sheet with parchment paper. Remove the truffle mixture from the refrigerator. Scoop balls from the mixture using a small cookie scoop or large melon baller. Roll into smooth balls and place on the prepared pan. Refrigerate for 30 minutes.

Top Pop Tip
To keep your hand steady when painting on the lines, rest your arm against the side of your workbench or table.

Step One
Melt the white candy coating wafers in a bowl over simmering water or in the microwave on the defrost setting. Remove from the heat.

Step Two
Remove the truffle pops from the refrigerator and insert a lollipop stick halfway into each. Dip and swirl each pop in the warm white candy coating to coat all over. Insert each lollipop stick in a block of Stryofoam and allow to dry for 15 minutes. If you wish, when the first coat has dried, dip the pop again in the white candy coating, which will give it a smoother finish and a more even color.

Step Three
When the candy coating has dried, roll out a piece of black fondant and cut out 6 small pentagons for each pop. Place them around the perimeter of the pop to resemble a soccer ball. Using a size 1 decorating tip, pipe a thin line of black decorating icing between the points of the pentagons. Melt the brown candy coating wafers over simmering water or in the microwave on the defrost setting, then brush the underside of each pop with the brown candy coating to look like mud. Set pops aside to dry in a cool place for 15 minutes. Will keep in an airtight container in the refrigerator for up to 3 days.

Silver Moon

These pops prove that the moon is not made of green cheese, but of delicious chocolate instead. Dip the truffles twice in the melted candy coating to get a smoother and more even finish.

POP BASE INGREDIENTS
White Chocolate and Rum Truffle Base, page 24

DECORATING INGREDIENTS
16 oz. (1 bag) gray candy coating wafers (plus more if necessary)
Paper lollipop sticks
4 oz. fondant, tinted gray
Edible silver glitter

TO MAKE THE SILVER MOON POPS
Line a baking sheet with parchment paper. Remove the truffle mixture from the refrigerator. Scoop balls from the mixture using a small cookie scoop or large melon baller. Form into smooth balls and place on the prepared pan. Place in the refrigerator for 30 minutes.

Step One
Melt the gray candy coating wafers in a bowl over simmering water or in the microwave on the defrost setting. Remove from the heat.

Step Two
Remove the truffle pops from the refrigerator and insert a lollipop stick halfway into each. Dip and swirl each pop in the warm gray candy coating. Insert each lollipop stick in a block of Styrofoam and let dry for 15 minutes. Keep the candy coating warm.

Step Three
Pinch off tiny pieces of fondant to create seven irregular craters for each moon. Attach them with melted gray candy coating. Sprinkle pops with edible silver glitter. Set aside to dry in a cool place for 15 minutes. Will keep in an airtight container in the refrigerator for up to 3 days.

Beach Ball

Recreate those happy beach afternoons of sun and sand with these colorful truffle pops. Vary the colors of melted candy coating, rolled fondant, and sprinkles, if you like.

POP BASE INGREDIENTS

**Hazelnut and Dark Chocolate
   Truffle Base, page 24**

DECORATING INGREDIENTS

8 oz. (½ bag) white candy coating
   wafers (more if necessary)
Paper lollipop sticks
4 oz. fondant, tinted blue
4 oz. fondant, tinted red
Edible glue or candy melt
1 oz. white gum paste

TO MAKE THE BEACH BALL POPS

Line a baking sheet with parchment paper. Remove the truffle mixture from the refrigerator. Scoop balls from the mixture using a small cookie scoop or large melon baller. Roll each into smooth balls and place on the prepared pan. Refrigerate for 30 minutes.

Step One

Melt the white candy coating wafers in a bowl over simmering water or in the microwave on the defrost setting. Remove from the heat.

Step Two

Remove the truffle pops from the refrigerator and insert a lollipop stick halfway into each. Dip and swirl each pop in the warm candy coating. Insert each lollipop stick in a block of Styrofoam and let dry for 15 minutes.

Step Three

Roll out the blue fondant to ⅛-inch (3-mm) thickness. Cut three leaf shapes, tapered at each end. Repeat with the red fondant. Attach stripes to each ball with edible glue. Dot edible glue or candy melt at the top of the beach ball and pat a circle of white gum paste on top. Set aside to dry in a cool place for 15 minutes. Will keep in an airtight container in the refrigerator for up to 3 days.

Friendly Ghost

**These spooky little ghosts hide a rich brownie secret under their sheets of white melted candy.
If you like, create different expressions for each ghost pop.**

POP BASE INGREDIENTS
Vegetable oil
Brownie Pop Base, page 27

DECORATING INGREDIENTS
Paper lollipop sticks
½ bag (8 oz.) white candy coating
wafers (more if necessary)
2 oz. fondant, tinted black
Edible glue

TO MAKE THE FRIENDLY GHOST POPS

Preheat the oven to 300°F (150°C). Brush each brownie mold cup with oil. Carefully spoon in the brownie batter so that each prepared cup is two-thirds full. (If you have only 1 brownie pop pan, do this in batches.) Bake for 15 minutes, remove from the oven, and insert a lollipop stick in the center of each brownie. Return to the oven and bake for 5–10 more minutes or until the brownies start to pull away from the sides of each cup. Carefully loosen brownies from the pan and turn out onto wire racks to cool completely.

Step One
Melt the white candy coating wafers in a bowl over simmering water or in the microwave on the defrost setting. Remove from the heat. Dip and swirl each brownie pop in the melted candy, then place them in a block of Styrofoam to cool for 15 minutes.

Step Two
Pinch off pieces of black fondant and press into ovals for eyes for each pop. Pinch off more pieces of black fondant and press into ovals for a mouth for each pop. Attach with edible glue. Using a toothpick, dab a little bit of the melted white candy coating onto the eyes to create a glint.

Step Three
Let pops cool completely in the block of Styrofoam for 15 minutes. Brownie pops will keep in a plastic container for up to 3 days.

Chocolate truffle zombie eyeball, see page 48; cookie spider web, see page 49

20 mins

makes 10-20

Zombie Eyeball

Eeeek! The zombies are out again! And they forgot to take their eyeballs with them. As you might guess, these are a favorite at children's parties.

POP BASE INGREDIENTS
Chocolate Truffle Base, page 24

DECORATING INGREDIENTS
8 oz. (½ bag) white candy coating wafers (more if necessary)
Paper lollipop sticks
4 oz. gum paste, tinted green
2 oz. gum paste, tinted black
Edible glue or candy melt
4 oz. gum paste, tinted red
Red licorice shoelace candy

TO MAKE THE ZOMBIE EYEBALL POPS
Line a baking sheet with parchment paper. Remove the truffle mixture from the refrigerator. Scoop balls from the mixture using a small cookie scoop or large melon baller. Roll into smooth balls and place on the prepared pan. Place in the refrigerator for 30 minutes.

Step One
Melt the white candy coating wafers in a bowl over simmering water or in the microwave on the defrost setting. Remove from the heat.

Step Two
Remove the truffle pops from the refrigerator and insert a lollipop stick halfway into each. Dip and swirl each pop in the warm white candy coating, leaving the underside of the ball uncovered. Insert each lollipop stick in a block of Styrofoam and let dry for 15 minutes.

Step Three
Roll out each color of gum paste to $1/16$-inch (1.5-mm) thickness. Using small round cookie cutters or a paring knife, cut a 1-inch (2.5-cm) diameter green circle for an iris and a smaller black circle for a pupil for each eyeball. Attach to each other and then to the truffle pop with edible glue. Cut a $3/4$-inch (2-cm) red fondant circle with a veiny border for the back of each eyeball and attach with edible glue or candy melt. Attach red shoelace candy to the back of each pop with candy melt. Set aside to dry in a cool place for 15 minutes. Will keep in an airtight container in the refrigerator for up to 3 days.

Spider Web

It's easy to get caught up in the sweet entanglement of these cookie pops. If you don't have a spider web cookie cutter, simply make a pattern on parchment paper and cut out the shapes with a paring knife.

POP BASE INGREDIENTS
Cookie Base, page 26

DECORATING INGREDIENTS
1 white cookie frosting, page 26
½ black cookie frosting, page 26
4 oz. fondant, tinted black
White sugar pearls
Edible black pen
Paper lollipop sticks

TO MAKE THE SPIDER WEB POPS
Preheat the oven to 400°F (200°C). On a lightly floured work surface, roll out the dough to ¼- to ½-inch (6.5- to 13-mm) thickness. Cut into shapes with a spider web cookie cutter. Place cookies 1 inch (2.5 cm) apart on ungreased cookie sheets. Bake for 6–8 minutes or until lightly browned at the edges. Transfer cookies to wire racks and let cool completely.

Step One
Pour half the white icing into a plastic squeeze bottle fitted with a size 2 round tip. Outline each cookie with the icing, then fill in the rest. Then tint the remaining icing black and pipe circles around the cookies, following the outline of the cookies' edges. Draw a toothpick from the center outward to create a feathered effect for the web. Let the cookies sit on wire racks for 1 hour.

Step Two
Pinch off small pieces of black fondant and create a ½-inch (1.25-cm) spider body and legs. Add white sugar pearls for the eyes and dot on black edible pen for the eyes. Attach to each cookie with some icing (or, if you prefer, use some edible glue). Let sit for 30 minutes.

Step Three
Attach a lollipop stick to the back of each cookie with icing and let the pops rest on a work surface until the stick is attached. Set the pops upright in a Styrofoam block. Will keep in an airtight container at room temperature for 1–2 weeks.

Sir Choc-a-Lot

Make these chocolate cake pops for the chess-mad friends in your life—or someone who knows every Knight of the Round Table. You'll be sure to win the day.

POP BASE INGREDIENTS
Chocolate Cake Base, page 21

DECORATING INGREDIENTS
8 oz. (½ bag) gray candy coating wafers (or white wafers tinted with a little black coloring)
Paper lollipop sticks
Edible silver paint
2 oz. fondant, tinted pink
2 oz. fondant, tinted yellow
Edible glue
Edible gold paint
Cocoa butter, melted
Edible black dusting powder

TO MAKE THE SIR CHOC-A-LOT POPS
Line a baking sheet with parchment paper. Using an ice cream scoop, scoop about 2 tablespoons Chocolate Cake Pop Base. Roll into a ball, then form into a helmet shape with a flat bottom. Place on the prepared baking sheet. Repeat the process with the remaining cake pop base. Cover the helmet shapes with plastic wrap and refrigerate for 30 minutes.

Step One
Melt the candy coating wafers in a bowl over simmering water or in the microwave on the defrost setting. Remove from the heat and let cool for 5 minutes. Meanwhile, remove the cake pops from the refrigerator and let rest for 5 minutes. Dip each lollipop stick about 1 inch (2.5 cm) deep in the melted candy coating, then insert it in the bottom of each cake pop. Place each cake pop, stick up, on the baking sheet. Set aside for 15 minutes at room temperature. Keep the candy coating warm.

Step Two
Once the candy coating has secured the stick, dip and swirl each cake pop in the warm candy coating. Insert each lollipop stick in a block of Styrofoam. Set aside in a cool place, not the refrigerator, for about 30 minutes while the coating sets.

Step Three
Paint the cake pop with the edible silver paint (or you can leave it gray, if you wish). Set aside to dry. Roll out the pink fondant on a plastic surface to ¹⁄₁₆-inch (1.5-mm) thickness. With a

paring knife, cut out curved T-shapes about 1 inch (2.5 cm) wide and ¾ inch (2 cm) long. Roll out the yellow fondant and cut out T-shaped frames for each face. Place a T-shaped frame over a face and then place the framed face on the front of each helmet, using melted candy coating or edible glue to make it adhere. With a narrow paintbrush, brush edible gold paint over the yellow face frame. Mix the melted cocoa butter with a little of the black dusting powder. With a paintbrush, paint on the eyes and the mouth. Place pops upright in the Styrofoam block. Will keep for up to 3 days at room temperature.

Derby Winner

Win, place, or show? Win, of course! These racehorse pops gallop to a first in flavor and presentation.

POP BASE INGREDIENTS
Chocolate Cake Base, page 21

DECORATING INGREDIENTS
8 oz. (½ bag) brown candy coating wafers (more if necessary)
Paper lollipop sticks
1 oz. gum paste, tinted pink
Edible glue
2 oz. fondant, tinted dark brown
2 oz. fondant, tinted light brown
2 oz. gum paste, tinted black
1 oz. fondant, tinted yellow
Cocoa butter, melted
Edible black dusting powder

TO MAKE THE DERBY WINNER POPS
Line a baking sheet with parchment paper. Using an ice cream scoop, scoop about 2 tablespoons Chocolate Cake Pop Base. Roll into a ball, then form into a horse's head shape with a flat bottom. Place on the prepared baking sheet. Repeat the process with the remaining cake pop base. Cover the baking sheet with plastic wrap and refrigerate for 30 minutes.

Top Pop Tip
To make the ears, roll the ball of fondant and flatten with the end of a rolling pin. Pinch one end together and then the other end. Cut the bottom off with a knife for a flat base.

Step One
Melt the brown candy coating wafers in a bowl over simmering water or in the microwave on the defrost setting. Remove from the heat and let cool for 5 minutes. Meanwhile, remove the cake pops from the refrigerator and let rest for 5 minutes. Dip each lollipop stick about 1 inch (2.5 cm) deep in the melted candy coating, then insert it in the bottom of each cake pop. Place each cake pop, stick up, on the baking sheet. Set aside for 15 minutes at room temperature. Keep the candy coating warm.

Step Two
Once the candy coating has secured the stick, dip and swirl each cake pop in the warm candy coating. Insert the lollipop sticks in a block of Styrofoam. Set aside in a cool place, but not the refrigerator, for about 30 minutes.

Step Three
Pinch off very small pieces of pink gum paste and form into ¼-inch (6.5-mm) long nostrils. Attach 2 to each pop with edible glue or melted candy coating. Pinch off small pieces of dark brown fondant and form into ears. Attach 2 to each pop with glue or candy coating. Roll out teardrop shapes with the light brown fondant,

flatten, and attach to the head to create the mane. Roll out the black gum paste to $1/16$-inch (1.5-mm) thickness, cut out $1/16$-inch (1.5 mm) wide strips for the harness, attach, and cut off any excess. Roll out little yellow fondant balls and attach for the buckles of the bit. With melted cocoa butter mixed with black edible dusting powder, paint on the eyes. Place pops upright in the Styrofoam block. Will keep for up to 3 days at room temperature.

Robot

C3PO and R2D2, you're wanted in the party room.

POP BASE INGREDIENTS
Yellow Cake Base, page 20

DECORATING INGREDIENTS
8 oz. (½ bag) gray candy coating wafers (more if necessary), or white wafers tinted with a little black coloring
Paper lollipop sticks
4 oz. gum paste, tinted yellow
Edible silver spray
Edible glue
Button candy on paper
Red sugar pearls
Cocoa butter, melted
Edible black dusting powder

TO MAKE THE ROBOT POPS
Line a baking sheet with parchment paper. With an ice cream scoop, scoop about 2 tablespoons Yellow Cake Pop Base, and divide it into three parts. Form two parts into a cube and roll the third part into a cylinder. Cut a corner out of the cube and cut the cylinder in half. Secure the cylinder into the cube with some melted candy coating and form into a robot head. Place on the prepared baking sheet. Repeat the process with the remaining cake pop base. Cover the baking tray with plastic wrap and refrigerate for 30 minutes.

> ### Top Pop Tip
> Wrap the lollipop stick with paper towel when spraying to prevent the edible silver spray from messing up the stick.

Step One
Melt the gray candy coating wafers in a bowl over simmering water or in the microwave on the defrost setting. Remove from the heat and let cool for 5 minutes. Meanwhile, remove the cake pops from the refrigerator and let rest for 5 minutes. Dip each lollipop stick about 1 inch (2.5 cm) deep in the melted candy coating, then insert it in the bottom of each cake pop. Place each cake pop, stick up, on the baking sheet. Set aside for 15 minutes at room temperature. Keep the candy coating warm.

Step Two
Once the candy coating has secured the stick, dip and swirl each cake pop in the warm candy coating. Insert the lollipop sticks in a block of Styrofoam. Set aside in a cool place, not the refrigerator, for about 30 minutes.

Step Three
Spray the pops with edible silver spray paint and allow to dry for 10 minutes. Roll out the yellow gum paste to ¹⁄₁₆-inch (1.5 mm) thickness. Using a paring knife, cut out a 1-inch (2.5-mm) long lightning bolt for each pop. Insert in the top of each pop. With the edible glue or melted candy coating, attach a button candy on each side for knobs. Glue on the red sugar pearls for eyes. Mix a little melted cocoa butter with a little black dusting powder, and create teeth lines with a fine paintbrush. Place pops upright in the Styrofoam block. Will keep for up to 3 days at room temperature.

Dinosaur

Millerosaurus. Jonesasaurus. If you make your own dinosaurs—especially the cake pop variety—you get to name the new species.

POP BASE INGREDIENTS
Chocolate Cake Base, page 21

DECORATING INGREDIENTS
8 oz. (½ bag) green candy coating
   wafers (more if necessary)
Paper lollipop sticks
2 oz. gum paste, tinted purple
2 oz. white gum paste
Edible glue
White sugar pearls
Cocoa butter, melted
Edible black dusting powder

TO MAKE THE DINOSAUR POPS
Line a baking sheet with parchment paper. Using an ice cream scoop, scoop about 2 tablespoons Chocolate Cake Pop Base. Form into a dinosaur head. Place on the prepared baking sheet. Repeat the process with the remaining cake pop base. Cover the baking sheet with plastic wrap and refrigerate for 30 minutes.

Step One
Melt the candy coating wafers in a bowl over simmering water or in the microwave on the defrost setting. Remove from the heat and let cool for 5 minutes. Meanwhile, remove the cake pops from the refrigerator and let rest for 5 minutes. Dip each lollipop stick about 1 inch (2.5 cm) deep in the melted candy coating, then insert it in the bottom of each cake pop. Place each cake pop, stick up, on the baking sheet. Let set for 15 minutes at room temperature. Keep the candy coating warm.

Step Two
Once the candy coating has secured the stick, dip and swirl each cake pop in the warm candy coating. Insert the lollipop sticks in a block of Styrofoam. Set aside in a cool place, not the refrigerator, for about 30 minutes.

Step Three
Roll out the purple gum paste and cut out 3 elongated pentagon shapes for each cake pop for the spines. With the white gum paste, roll out a horn for each pop. Attach them all to the dinosaur heads with edible glue or melted candy coating. Glue on white sugar pearls for eyes. With the melted cocoa butter mixed with black edible dusting powder, paint on the pupils of the eyes, eyebrows, and nostrils. Place pops upright in the Styrofoam block. Will keep for up to 3 days at room temperature.

Dinosaur Egg

No trip to the natural history museum is as exciting as finding dinosaur eggs—at home or at a gathering. Make these for the child who is *really, really* into everything dinosaurs.

POP BASE INGREDIENTS
Yellow Cake Base, page 20

DECORATING INGREDIENTS
8 oz. (½ bag) yellow candy coating wafers (more if necessary)
Paper lollipop sticks
2 oz. gum paste, tinted purple
Edible glue
Cocoa butter, melted
Edible black dusting powder

TO MAKE THE DINOSAUR EGG POPS
Line a baking sheet with parchment paper. Using an ice cream scoop, scoop about 2 tablespoons Yellow Cake Pop Base. Shape into a dinosaur egg. Place on the prepared baking sheet. Repeat the process with the remaining cake pop base. Cover the baking sheet with plastic wrap and refrigerate for 30 minutes.

Step One
Melt the candy coating wafers in a bowl over simmering water or in the microwave on the defrost setting. Remove from the heat and let cool for 5 minutes. Meanwhile, remove the cake pops from the refrigerator and let rest for 5 minutes. Dip each lollipop stick about 1 inch (2.5 cm) deep in the melted candy coating, then insert it in the bottom of each cake pop. Place each cake pop, stick up, on the baking sheet. Let set for 15 minutes at room temperature. Keep the candy coating warm.

Step Two
Once the candy coating has secured the stick, dip and swirl each cake pop in the warm candy coating. Insert the lollipop sticks in a block of Styrofoam. Set aside in a cool place, not the refrigerator, for about 30 minutes.

Step Three
Pinch off small pieces of purple gum paste and form into 5½-inch (1.25-cm) long ovals for each pop. Attach with edible glue or melted candy coating. Mix melted cocoa butter with a little black dusting powder. With a fine paintbrush, paint on the egg cracks. Place pops upright in the Styrofoam block. Will keep for up to 3 days at room temperature.

Wicked Witch

Just ask Snow White or Dorothy from *The Wizard of Oz*—you want wicked witches to disappear quickly. With these toothsome pops, that's never a problem. If you can't find black candy coating wafers, use a half-and-half mixture of blue and red, then stir in a little black food coloring after the wafers have melted.

POP BASE INGREDIENTS

Vegetable oil
Chocolate Brownie Base, page 27

DECORATING INGREDIENTS

Paper lollipop sticks
½ bag (8 oz.) spooky green candy coating wafers (or mix some blue and yellow candy coating wafers)
Red licorice shoelace candy
2 oz. black gum paste
Store-bought mini-ice cream cones
½ bag (8 oz.) black candy coating wafers (or mix red and blue wafers with black food coloring)

2 oz. fondant, tinted light brown
2 oz. yellow gum paste
Candy melt
4 oz. fondant, tinted green
White sugar pearls
Cocoa butter, melted
Edible black dusting powder

TO MAKE THE WICKED WITCH POPS

Preheat the oven to 300°F (150°C). Brush each brownie mold cup with oil. Carefully spoon in the brownie batter so that each prepared cup is two-thirds full. (If you have only 1 brownie pop pan, do this in batches.) Bake for 15 minutes, remove from the oven, and insert a lollipop stick in the center of each brownie. Return to the oven and bake for 5–10 more minutes or until the brownies start to pull away from the sides of each cup. Carefully loosen brownies from the pan and turn out onto wire racks to cool completely.

Step One

Melt the spooky green candy wafers in a bowl over simmering water or in the microwave on the defrost setting. Remove from the heat. Dip and swirl each brownie pop in the melted candy, then place in a block of Styrofoam. Attach lengths of red shoelace candy for hair. Let cool for 15 minutes.

Step Two

Roll out the black gum paste to ¹⁄₁₆-inch (1.5-mm) thickness, then with a round cutter cut out 2-inch (5-cm) circles to form the rim of the witch's hat. Attach to the top of the head with melted candy coating. Carefully trim each ice cream cone until it measures 2 inches (5 cm) long. Melt the black candy coating wafers in a bowl over simmering water or in the microwave on the defrost setting. Remove from the heat. Using tongs, dip and swirl each cone in the melted black candy, then set it on top of the hat rim to make the hat. Repeat until all pops have their hats. Roll out the light brown fondant to ¹⁄₁₆-inch (1.5-mm) thickness and

cut out strips to wrap around the base of the hat. Roll out the yellow flower paste to ¹⁄₁₆-inch (1.5-mm) thickness and cut out the hat buckles. Attach both to the hats with either edible glue or melted candy coating.

Step Three

Pinch off pieces of green fondant to create a big nose for each pop. Attach with candy melt. Attach white sugar pearls for the eyes, and create the pupils by painting on melted cocoa butter mixed with black edible dusting powder. Let pops cool completely. Brownie pops will keep in a plastic container for up to 3 days.

Mug of Hot Chocolate

With a cup of coffee in the morning or a mug of hot chocolate before bed, these clever pops are a great way to start or end your day. They're also scrumptious treats to bring to a neighborhood gathering.

POP BASE INGREDIENTS

Vegetable oil
Chocolate Brownie Base, page 27

DECORATING INGREDIENTS

1 cup (6 oz.) semisweet chocolate chips
Paper lollipop sticks
7 oz. white fondant
1 oz. white candy coating wafers
Miniature marshmallows
Edible glue
Tiny sugar flowers

TO MAKE THE MUG OF HOT CHOCOLATE POPS

Preheat the oven to 300°F (150°C). Brush each brownie mold cup with oil. Carefully spoon in the brownie batter so that each prepared cup is two-thirds full. (If you have only 1 brownie pop pan, do this in batches.) Bake for 20–25 minutes or until the brownies start to pull away from the sides of each cup. Carefully loosen brownies from the cups and turn out onto wire racks to cool completely.

> ### Top Pop Tip
> Make the fondant handles a day in advance and leave out to dry. This will make them easier to attach.

Step One

Cut ¼ inch (6.5 mm) off the top and bottom of each brownie and discard. Turn the trimmed brownie upside down and set aside on a work surface.

Step Two

Melt the chocolate chips in a bowl over simmering water or in the microwave on the defrost setting. Remove from the heat.
Dip each lollipop stick about 1 inch (2.5 cm) deep into the melted chocolate and insert it in the bottom of each pop. Let cool for 15 minutes upside down on a work surface. Keep the melted chocolate warm.

Step Three

Roll out the white fondant to ⅛-inch (3-mm) thickness. Cut strips large enough to wrap all the way around each brownie. Leave a little extra at the top and the bottom. Fold the fondant under the brownie bottom, and smooth off the sides of the fondant. Melt the white candy coating wafers. Spoon or swirl the melted semisweet chocolate on top of each brownie pop to create the hot chocolate. With a toothpick or skewer, create a white swirl with some of the melted white candy coating. Attach 3 miniature marshmallows to the chocolate while it is still hot. Roll out small cylinders of the white fondant and, with edible glue, attach to the side of the brownie to create a handle. Attach tiny sugar flowers to the sides of each "cup" with edible glue. Let dry.

Baby's Rattle

These are delightful to make for a baby shower. You can make them half blue and half white, as discussed here, or all pink or all blue if the parents know whether they're having a girl or boy.

POP BASE INGREDIENTS
Espresso Bean Truffle Base, page 24

DECORATING INGREDIENTS
8 oz. (½ bag) pink candy coating wafers (more if necessary)
8 oz. (½ bag) pale blue candy coating wafers, or white tinted with blue food coloring (more if necessary)
Paper lollipop sticks
4 oz. white fondant
Heart-shaped sprinkles
Edible glue
Ribbon

TO MAKE THE BABY'S RATTLE POPS
Line a baking sheet with parchment paper. Remove the truffle mixture from the refrigerator. Scoop balls from the mixture using a small cookie scoop or large melon baller. Roll into smooth balls and place on the prepared pan. Place in the refrigerator for 30 minutes.

Step One
Place the pink and blue candy coating wafers in separate small glass bowls over two saucepans of hot water. Heat over low heat, stirring, until coating has melted. Remove from the heat.

Step Two
Remove the truffle pops from the refrigerator and insert a lollipop stick halfway into each. Dip the pops in the blue candy coating. Insert each lollipop stick in a Styrofoam block and let dry for 15 minutes. Once the candy coating has set, dip the top half of the pop into the pink candy coating. Replace the pops in the Styrofoam and let dry for 15 minutes more.

Step Three
Roll out the fondant to ⅛-inch (3-mm) thickness. Using a paring knife, cut ½-inch (1.25-cm) wide strips of fondant to reach around each truffle. Attach strip to the ball with edible glue. Attach the tiny hearts to the fondant strip with the glue. Set pops aside to dry in a cool place for 15 minutes, then tie a tiny, pretty ribbon bow around each stick. Will keep in a cool, dry place (not the refrigerator) for up to 3 days.

Cookie baby doll, see page 66; yellow cake rubber ducky, see page 67

Baby Doll

These baby-faced cookie pops won't make a fuss during a first birthday party or a baby shower. Allow a little extra time to bake these, unless you have several round cookie pop pans.

POP BASE INGREDIENTS
Vegetable oil
See Cookie Base, page 26

DECORATING INGREDIENTS
Paper lollipop sticks
2 oz. fondant, tinted pale pink
Edible glue
2 oz. fondant, tinted pale blue
2 oz. white fondant
2 oz. fondant, tinted black
Cocoa butter, melted
Edible black dusting powder

TO MAKE THE BABY DOLL POPS
Preheat the oven to 400°F (200°C). Brush the inside of the cookie pop pan with oil. Pinch off 4 pieces of dough, flatten slightly on a floured surface, and press into each cookie pop mold, filling up to ⅛ inch (3 mm) from the top edge. Gently slide in each lollipop stick. Bake for 6–8 minutes or until lightly browned at the edges. Let cool in the pan for 1 minute, then carefully invert onto wire racks to cool completely. Repeat the process with the remaining dough.

Step One
When the cookies are cool, roll out the pink fondant on a plastic surface to ⅛-inch (3-mm) thickness. With a round cookie cutter, cut out a circle about ³⁄₁₆ inch (5 mm) less in diameter than the cookie. Attach it to the cookie with edible glue. Roll out a pink fondant ball for the nose, and attach it to the face.

Step Two
Roll out the blue fondant to ⅕-inch (6 mm) thickness and cut it into the shape of a baby's pacifier. Roll 2 blue cylinders to add to the pacifier shape. With edible glue, attach the parts of the pacifier to each other and then

to the cookie. Cut strips of the blue fondant for the bow (see page 108), and attach to the cookie with edible glue. Roll out the white fondant, cut out circles for the eyes, and attach with edible glue. Roll out the black fondant and cut out smaller circles as pupils. Attach the pupils with edible glue. Paint on eyelashes with melted cocoa butter mixed with edible black dusting powder.

Step Three
Let the cookies set, then place them upright in a Styrofoam block. Will keep in an airtight container for 1 week.

Rubber Ducky

**Rub-a-dub-dub, but don't take these near the tub. They're meant for fun.
You can always wash up later.**

POP BASE INGREDIENTS
Yellow Cake Base, page 20

DECORATING INGREDIENTS
**8 oz. (½ bag) yellow candy melts
  (more if necessary)
Paper lollipop sticks
4 oz. fondant, tinted orange
Edible glue
White sugar pearls
Cocoa butter, melted
Edible black dusting powder**

TO MAKE THE RUBBER DUCKY POPS
Line a baking sheet with parchment paper. Using an ice cream scoop, scoop about 2 tablespoons Yellow Cake Pop Base. Divide into a larger and a smaller piece to create the duck's head and body. Place on the prepared baking sheet. Repeat the process with the remaining cake pop base. Cover the baking sheet with plastic wrap and refrigerate for 30 minutes.

Step One
Melt the candy coating wafers in a bowl over simmering water or in the microwave on the defrost setting. Remove from the heat and let cool for 5 minutes. Meanwhile, remove the cake pops from the refrigerator and let rest for 5 minutes. Dip each lollipop stick about 1 inch (2.5 cm) deep in the melted candy coating, then insert it in the bottom of each of the larger-sized cake balls. Place these pops, stick up, on the baking sheet. Let set for 15 minutes at room temperature. Keep the candy coating warm.

Step Two
Once the candy coating has secured the stick, dip the smaller cake piece (the duck's head) into a little bit of the warm candy coating and secure to the cake pop (the duck's body). Insert the lollipop sticks in a block of Styrofoam and wait for the candy coating to set. Once it has set, dip and swirl each cake pop in the warm candy coating. Insert the lollipop sticks in the Styrofoam block and set aside in a cool place, not the refrigerator, for about 30 minutes.

Step Three
Roll out a small piece of the orange fondant and shape it into a duck's beak. With your fingers, make the bill wider where it attaches to the head and thinner at the mouth end. Attach the beak to the duck with a little warm candy coating or edible glue. Attach the white sugar pearls for the eyes. Paint on pupils with a little melted cocoa butter mixed with black edible dusting powder. Place pops upright in the Styrofoam block. Will keep for up to 3 days at room temperature.

Lavender Heart

A little lavender in the toffee makes these hearts extra special. You will need heart-shaped cookie pop pans for this recipe.

POP BASE INGREDIENTS
Vegetable oil
Chewy Lavender Toffee Base,
    page 29

DECORATING INGREDIENTS
Edible glue
Lavender sugar pearls or
    sprinkles
4 oz. white candy coating wafers
Red and blue food colorings
Paper lollipop sticks

TO MAKE THE LAVENDER HEART POPS
Brush the inside of each cookie pop mold with oil. Place the lollipop sticks so that they reach to the center of each mold. Carefully divide the hot toffee among the prepared molds so that the lollipop sticks are fully covered. Let cool completely.

Step One
Remove from the molds. Place a small heart-shaped cookie cutter over the toffee heart and brush the inside with edible glue. Sprinkle glue with the lavender sugar pearls or sprinkles and press down with the end of a paintbrush.

Step Two
Melt the candy coating wafers in a bowl over simmering water or in the microwave on the defrost setting. Remove the melted candy coating from the heat and add red and blue food colorings to create a lavender hue. Using a fine paintbrush or a piping bag fitted with a small round tip, brush or pipe a lavender border on each heart.

Step Three
Set the pops in a Styrofoam block to dry in a cool place for 15 minutes. Will keep in a cool, dry place (not the refrigerator) for up to 1 week.

Marshmallow heartthrob, see page 70; honeycomb winged heart, see page 71

Heartthrob

A secret love? A romantic secret? The key to your heart? The coded message is in this pop.

POP BASE INGREDIENTS
2 cups confectioners' sugar
Rose Marshmallow Base, page 25
Vegetable oil

DECORATING INGREDIENTS
Confectioners' sugar for dusting
Purple or colored sprinkles
Candy hearts
Edible glue
Paper lollipop sticks

TO MAKE THE HEARTTHROB POPS
Sift half of the confectioners' sugar onto a work surface and half onto a baking sheet. Invert the 9 x 13-inch (22 x 33-cm) marshmallow base onto the prepared work surface; remove the parchment. Brush the inside of a 2-inch (5-cm) wide heart-shaped cookie cutter with vegetable oil. Cut out hearts and place them on the prepared baking sheet, dusting lightly with confectioners' sugar. Brush the cutter with oil as necessary to keep the marshmallow from sticking.

Step One
Using a very small heart-shaped cutter, cut a small central heart out of each large one. Put the sprinkles on a plate. Dredge the sticky sides of each small heart in sprinkles and press back into the large heart.

Step Two
Attach a candy heart to the center of the marshmallow heart with edible glue. Insert a lollipop stick into each pop. Insert pops in a block of Styrofoam to dry. Marshmallow pops will keep for 3 days stored in a plastic container.

Honeycomb | 10 mins | makes 8

Winged Heart

**Send a very romantic message with winged heart pops made with bubbly honeycomb candy.
Use heart-shaped cookie pop pans to make these pops.**

POP BASE INGREDIENTS
Vegetable oil
Paper lollipop sticks
Honeycomb Base, page 23

DECORATING INGREDIENTS
Candy heart-shaped sprinkles
4 oz. white candy coating wafers
Red food coloring
1 sugar sheet
Edible glue

TO MAKE THE WINGED HEART POPS
Brush the inside of each cookie pop mold with oil. Place the lollipop sticks so that they reach to the center of each mold. Carefully and evenly pour the hot honeycomb candy into the oiled molds so that the lollipop sticks are fully covered.

Step One
Place heart sprinkles around the perimeter of each hot star. Let cool completely in a dry room.

Step Two
Remove from the molds. Melt the candy coating wafers in a bowl over simmering water or in the microwave on the defrost setting. Remove from the heat and stir in red food coloring to tint the candy coating hot pink. Brush or pipe the melted candy around the perimeter of each heart. Cut a pair of Cupid's wings from a sugar sheet for each heart pop and attach them with edible glue. Set pops in a Styrofoam block to dry in a dry place. Will keep at dry room temperature for 1 day or in an airtight container for 1 week.

Snowman

Let it snow! These marshmallow snowmen love getting together and swapping tales of blizzards, ice skating, and the inevitable thaw.

POP BASE INGREDIENTS
Marshmallow Base, page 25
2 cups confectioners' sugar

DECORATING INGREDIENTS
6 oz. white chocolate chips
6 oz. (⅓ bag) red candy coating wafers, tinted red
Paper lollipop sticks
1 oz. fondant, tinted orange
6 oz. fondant, tinted red
Black sugar pearls
Edible pink dusting powder

TO MAKE THE SNOWMAN POPS
Use small and large half-sphere silicone molds to make the marshmallow base, as described on page 25. When the marshmallow has firmed, sift the confectioners' sugar onto a work surface. Invert the marshmallow half spheres onto the prepared work surface.

Top Pop Tip
Use a clean ruler to cut the shape of the scarf.

Step One
Melt the white chocolate chips in a bowl over simmering water or in the microwave using the defrost setting. Melt the candy wafers in a bowl over simmering water.

Step Two
Assemble snowmen by attaching 2 large half spheres with the melted white chocolate, sandwiching a lollipop stick between them. The stick should poke out the top by about ⅔ inch (1.75 cm). With melted white chocolate, attach 2 smaller half spheres on top, with the top of the lollipop stick between them. Place the snowmen upright in a Styrofoam block to dry for 30 minutes. Keep the chocolate warm. Dip the head of the snowman in the red candy melt.

Step Three
Pinch off small pieces of orange fondant and form a carrot nose. Attach it to the snowman's head with melted white chocolate. Roll out the red fondant to ⅛-inch (3-mm) thickness. Cut out 6-inch (15-cm) long red scarves and wrap around each snowman, securing with the melted chocolate. Fashion the hat out of red fondant and attach with red candy melt. Attach black sugar pearls for eyes and for buttons. With a dry brush, brush on rosy cheeks with the pink dusting powder. Set snowmen aside to dry for 15 minutes. These marshmallow pops will keep for 1 day in a cool, dry place.

Rose marshmallow arctic explorer, see page 74; cinnamon spice marshmallow Christmas pudding, see page 75

Arctic Explorer

Where's my bobsled? Where did the huskies go? They're all back at the igloo.

POP BASE INGREDIENTS
2 cups confectioners' sugar
Rose Marshmallow Base, page 25 (in half-sphere silicone molds)
Marshmallow Base, page 25 (in square silicone baking pan)

DECORATING INGREDIENTS
8 oz. (½ bag) white candy coating wafers
Paper lollipop sticks
8 oz. (½ bag) blue candy coating wafers
4 oz. fondant, tinted black
Edible glue
White sugar polka dots
Edible black pen
Edible pink dusting powder

TO MAKE THE ARCTIC EXPLORER POPS
Sift the confectioners' sugar onto a work surface. Invert the half spheres of Rose Marshmallow Base and the square silicone baking pan of Marshmallow Base onto the prepared surface.

Step One
Melt the white candy coating wafers in a bowl over simmering water or in the microwave using the defrost setting. With the melted white candy, attach the half spheres to make a ball, sandwiching a lollipop stick between them. Set aside in a Styrofoam block for 10 minutes. Melt the blue candy coating wafers in a bowl over simmering water or in the microwave using the defrost setting. Dip the backs of the marshmallow spheres into the blue candy coating to create a hood. Let dry in a block of Styrofoam for 10 minutes.

Step Two
Melt the white marshmallow from the square pan in a bowl over simmering water or in the microwave using the defrost setting. Spoon the melted marshmallow into a piping bag fitted with a small round tip. Pipe a "furry" border around each marshmallow ball.

Step Three
Pinch off pieces of black fondant and make a mouth for each face. Attach with edible glue. Attach white sugar polka dot eyes with edible glue. Paint on pupils and eyebrows with edible black pen. With a dry brush, brush on rosy cheeks with the pink dusting powder. Insert in the Styrofoam block to dry for 15 minutes. These marshmallow pops will keep for 1 day in a cool, dry place (the fondant prevents them from being put in plastic to keep for longer—the fondant will absorb the moisture from the marshmallow and melt).

Marsh Mallow · 15 mins · makes 12-24

Christmas Pudding

The fondant-covered fruitcake known as Christmas pudding is an old English holiday tradition.
Serve these fun versions at a holiday caroling party or after you've read or watched Charles Dickens'
A Christmas Carol.

POP BASE INGREDIENTS

2 cups confectioners' sugar
Cinnamon Spice Marshmallow Base,
　　page 25 (in silicone mini-muffin
　　pans)

DECORATING INGREDIENTS

6 oz. semisweet chocolate chips
Paper lollipop sticks
4 oz. white fondant
1 oz. fondant, tinted green
1 oz. fondant, tinted red

TO MAKE THE CHRISTMAS PUDDING POPS

Sift the confectioners' sugar onto a work surface. Invert the firm marshmallows from silicone mini-muffin pans onto the prepared work surface. Dust lightly with confectioners' sugar.

Step One

Melt the chocolate chips in a bowl over simmering water or in the microwave using the defrost setting. Dip the tip of each lollipop stick into the melted chocolate, then insert a lollipop stick into each pop. Now dip the whole pop in the melted chocolate to coat. Insert pops in a block of Styrofoam to dry for 15 minutes.

Step Two

Roll out the white fondant to ⅛-inch (3-mm) thickness and cut out a 1-inch (2.5-cm) scalloped icing circle for each pop. Attach with some melted chocolate. Roll out the green fondant to ⅛-inch (3-mm) thickness and cut out ¼-inch (6.5-mm) holly leaves. Pinch off small pieces of red fondant and roll into 2 holly berries for each pop. Set aside to dry for 15 minutes. Marshmallow pops will keep for 3 days stored in a plastic container.

Marsh Mallow · 30 mins · makes 12-24

Fruit Kebabs

Slices of kiwi and orange meet in the middle with a cube of pineapple—all created with homemade marshmallow. Serve these whimsical kebabs with a sweet dip made from cream cheese and confectioners' sugar.

POP BASE INGREDIENTS
**Citrus Marshmallow Base,
page 25**

DECORATING INGREDIENTS
**1 cup granulated sugar, tinted
lime-green
1 cup granulated sugar, tinted
orange
1 cup granulated sugar, tinted
light orange
1 cup granulated sugar, tinted
yellow
1 cup white sugar
Vegetable oil
Edible glue
Black sugar pearls
2 oz. white chocolate, melted
Paper lollipop sticks**

TO MAKE THE FRUIT KEBAB POPS
Place a sheet of baking parchment on a work surface. Invert the marshmallow base from two 8-inch (20-cm) silicone dishes onto the prepared work surface.

Step One
Place the colored sugars onto 5 small plates. Put the white sugar on another plate. Brush a 1-inch (2.5-cm) round cutter with oil. Cut out 12 marshmallow circles, then cover the sticky edges with the lime-green sugar. Brush edible glue onto the flat sides of the circles and sprinkle with the white and the light lime-green sugars, then stick on black sugar pearls to create kiwi slices.

Step Two
Using an oiled 2-inch (5-cm) round cutter, cut out 6 marshmallow circles, then cut them in half and roll the curved sticky edges in the orange sugar. Create "segments" on the orange-edged half-circles by brushing them with edible glue, leaving lines in between the "segments." Sprinkle the glue with the light orange sugar and shake off any excess.

Step Three
Cut out 12 cubes from the remaining marshmallow and roll them in the yellow sugar. Brush on edible glue anywhere the sugar has not stuck and sprinkle on more yellow sugar. Carefully thread 3 different "fruits" onto each lollipop stick, using white melted chocolate to secure them if necessary. Insert lollipop sticks in a Styrofoam block to dry for 15 minutes. Marshmallow pops will keep for 3 days stored in a plastic container.

Marsh Mallow · **20 mins** · *makes 12-24*

Baby Blocks

For a preschool party or a baby shower, these soft and squishy pops can spell "yum" with ease.

POP BASE INGREDIENTS
Citrus Marshmallow Base, page 25

DECORATING INGREDIENTS
8 oz. (½ bag) red candy coating wafers
8 oz. (½ bag) blue candy coating wafers
8 oz. (½ bag) green candy coating wafers
8 oz. (½ bag) yellow candy coating wafers
Paper lollipop sticks

TO MAKE THE BABY BLOCKS MARSHMALLOW POPS
Place a sheet of baking parchment on a work surface. Invert the marshmallow base from two 8-inch (20-cm) square silicone baking dishes onto the prepared work surface. Using a paring knife warmed in a cup of hot water, cut 1½-inch (4-cm) marshmallow squares.

Step One
Melt the candy coating wafers separately, in bowls over simmering water or in the microwave using the defrost setting. Carefully thread 3 marshmallow blocks onto a lollipop stick, using some yellow candy coating to secure the block if necessary. Fill a piping bag, fitted with a No. 2 tip, with one color of the melted candy coatings. Carefully pipe lines along the sides of the first marshmallow cube and write a letter in the center of all 4 vertical sides. Repeat the process with the second color in a different piping bag, and then with the third. You can insert the lollipop stick in a block of Styrofoam as you work if it makes it easier for you.

Step Two
Place the completed pops upright in a Styrofoam block to dry for 30 minutes. Marshmallow pops will keep for 3 days stored in a plastic container.

Marsh Mallow · 20 mins · makes 12-24

Cupcakes

These frosted cupcakes are all light, airy, whimsical fun. If you like, tint the mini-marshmallow "frosting" a different color as well.

POP BASE INGREDIENTS

2 cups confectioners' sugar
Rose Marshmallow Base in mini-muffin pans, page 25
½ Rose Marshmallow Base from square silicone baking dish, page 25

DECORATING INGREDIENTS

6 oz. semisweet or milk chocolate chips
Paper lollipop sticks
Sugar sprinkles

TO MAKE THE CUPCAKE POPS

Sift the confectioners' sugar onto a work surface. Invert the firm marshmallow shapes from the pans onto the prepared work surface; remove any parchment.

Top Pop Tip

Practice piping the marshmallow on a piece of baking paper first. To prevent the top from flattening, pipe a small amount of marshmallow into the center first and then pipe around and on top of the pop to build up the frosting top.

Step One

Melt the chocolate chips in a bowl over simmering water or in the microwave using the defrost setting. Insert a lollipop stick into each marshmallow muffin, then dip the pop in the melted chocolate to coat. Insert pops in a Styrofoam block to dry for 30 minutes.

Step Two

Melt the marshmallow from the silicone baking dish in a bowl over simmering water or in the microwave using the defrost setting. Spoon the melted marshmallow into a piping bag fitted with an open star nozzle. Pipe the frosting on each cupcake. Decorate with sugar sprinkles.

Step Three

Place the marshmallow pops in the Styrofoam block to dry for 15 minutes. Marshmallow pops will keep for 3 days stored in a plastic container.

Ahoy, Mate!

This sailor is walking the plank into... your mouth. He's delicious as a brownie pop, but he could work equally well as a chocolate cake pop.

POP BASE INGREDIENTS
Vegetable oil
Chocolate Mint Brownie Base, page 27

DECORATING INGREDIENTS
8 oz. (½ bag) skin tone candy coating wafers, or more as needed (mix pink and white candy coating wafers with a little yellow candy coating wafers)
Paper lollipop sticks
8 oz. (½ bag) white candy coating wafers

2 oz. gum paste, tinted black
White sugar polka dots
Cocoa butter, melted
Edible black dusting powder
Edible yellow dusting powder
Edible brown dusting powder
Edible pink dusting powder

HOW TO MAKE THE AHOY, MATE! POPS
Preheat the oven to 350°F (175°C). Brush each brownie mold cup with oil. Carefully spoon in the brownie batter so that each prepared cup is two thirds full. (If you have only 1 brownie pop pan, do this in 3 batches.) Bake for 20–25 minutes or until the brownies start to pull away from the sides of each cup. Carefully loosen from the pan and turn out onto wire racks to cool completely.

Step One
Cut ½ inch (1.25 cm) off the top of each brownie and discard. Cut ½ inch (1.25 cm) off the base of each brownie and set aside. Melt the skin tone candy coating wafers in a bowl over simmering water or in the microwave on the defrost setting. Remove from the heat. Dip each lollipop stick into the melted candy coating and insert in the bottom of each pop. Let cool for 15 minutes upside down on a work surface. Keep the melted candy warm. Dip and swirl each trimmed brownie pop in the skin tone candy, then insert sticks in a Styrofoam block to cool for 15 minutes.

Step Two
Melt the white candy coating wafers in a bowl over simmering water or in the microwave on the defrost setting. Remove from the heat. Attach the reserved brownie base to the top of the pop with some candy coating to form a sailor's cap. Let set for 5 minutes. Dip the pop into the white candy coating so the sailor's cap is fully coated. Let cool for 15 minutes in a Styrofoam block.

Step Three
Roll out the black gum paste and cut out a semicircle for the cap's brim and a band to wrap around the base. Attach with warm white candy coating. Attach white sugar polka dots for the eyes with a dot of warm candy coating. With a brush draw on pupils, eyebrows, and a mouth with the melted cocoa butter mixed with black dusting powder. Paint on an anchor on the front of the cap with yellow dusting powder mixed with melted cocoa butter. Paint hair with brown dusting powder mixed with melted cocoa butter. With a dry brush, brush on rosy cheeks with pink dusting powder. Leave in the block of Styrofoam to cool completely. Brownie pops will keep in a plastic container for up to 3 days.

Citrus marshmallow tugboat, see page 84; chocolate cake deep sea diver, see page 85

Tugboat

Ahoy, mate! These sweet treats can rescue a boy's birthday party or say "bon voyage" to adventurous friends.

POP BASE INGREDIENTS
Citrus Marshmallow Base, page 25

DECORATING INGREDIENTS
1 cup granulated sugar, tinted blue
1 cup granulated sugar, tinted red
Vegetable oil
Edible glue
Black sugar pearls
12 paper lollipop sticks

TO MAKE THE TUGBOAT POPS
Place a sheet of parchment paper on a work surface. Invert the marshmallow base onto the prepared work surface; remove the top parchment (if you used it).

Top Pop Tip
Rub your fingers with a mixture of corn starch and confectioners' sugar so that it is easier to handle the marshmallow.

Step One
Place the colored sugars on separate plates. Using a knife warmed in hot water or an oiled oval cutter, cut out 12 marshmallow boat bottoms. Roll all over in red sugar. Brush with edible glue and sprinkle on extra red sugar. With more oiled cutters or a warmed knife, cut 12 small cubes and 12 small circles from the remaining marshmallow. Roll the small circles in blue sugar.

Step Two
Stack the shapes together, using edible glue, to form a tugboat—the red on the bottom, the white cube in the middle, and the blue circle on top. Using edible glue, attach black sugar pearls for windows.

Step Three
Carefully thread a tugboat onto each lollipop stick, using edible glue to secure the boat if necessary. Place in a Styrofoam block to dry for 15 minutes. Marshmallow pops will keep for 3 days stored in a plastic container.

Chocolate Cake   20 mins   makes 22-26

Deep Sea Diver

Looking for undersea treasures among the ancient shipwrecks? Or a new marine species? If you make the pop, you can choose the adventure.

POP BASE INGREDIENTS
Chocolate Cake Base, page 21

DECORATING INGREDIENTS
8 oz. (½ bag) brown candy coating wafers (more if necessary)
Paper lollipop sticks
2 oz. fondant, tinted pink
2 oz. fondant, tinted light brown
Edible glue
Cocoa butter, melted
Edible black dusting powder
Edible gold paint

TO MAKE THE DEEP SEA DIVER POPS
Line a baking sheet with parchment paper. Using an ice cream scoop, scoop about 2 tablespoons Chocolate Cake Pop Base. Form into a ball. Place on the prepared baking sheet. Repeat the process with the remaining cake pop base. Cover the baking sheet with plastic wrap and refrigerate for 30 minutes.

Top Pop Tip
If you have any air bubbles after dipping in the candy melt, pop them with a toothpick and tap the pop on the side of a bowl to smooth out the candy coating.

Step One
Melt the candy coating wafers in a bowl over simmering water or in the microwave on the defrost setting. Remove from the heat and let cool for 5 minutes. Meanwhile, remove the cake pops from the refrigerator and let rest for 5 minutes. Dip each lollipop stick about 1 inch (2.5 cm) deep in the melted candy coating, then insert it in the bottom of each cake pop. Place each cake pop, stick up, on the baking sheet. Set aside for 15 minutes at room temperature. Keep the candy coating warm.

Step Two
Once the candy coating has secured the stick, dip and swirl each cake pop in the warm candy coating. Insert the lollipop sticks in a block of Styrofoam. Set aside in a cool place, not the refrigerator, for about 30 minutes.

Step Three
Roll out the pink fondant to ¹/₁₆-inch (1.5-mm) thickness. Using a paring knife, cut a 1-inch (2.5-cm) wide oval to make the pop's face. Roll out the light brown fondant and cut out the frame for the face. Attach it to the face, then attach the framed face with edible glue or melted candy coating to the pop. Create ½-inch (1.25-cm) diameter balls from the light brown fondant, flatten, and with a modeling tool indent a hole in each ball. Attach these with candy coating to the sides of the pop. Roll out 2 smaller balls, flatten one, and attach it to the top of the pop. Attach the other one on top. With the melted cocoa butter mixed with black edible dusting powder, paint on the eyes. Paint on the rivets with edible gold paint. Place upright in the Styrofoam block. Repeat the process with the other pops. Will keep for up to 3 days at room temperature.

Mouse

Why is it that mice feature so prominently in fairy tales and fantasy fiction? Maybe because they're so resourceful. Angelina Ballerina and Mrs. Tittlemouse represent only a few models for your creativity.

POP BASE INGREDIENTS
Yellow Cake Base, page 20

DECORATING INGREDIENTS
8 oz. (½ bag) pink candy coating wafers (more if necessary)
Paper lollipop sticks
2 oz. fondant, tinted pale pink
Edible glue
1 oz. fondant, tinted dark pink
White sugar pearls
Cocoa butter, melted
Edible black dusting powder

TO MAKE THE MOUSE POPS
Line a baking sheet with parchment paper. Using an ice cream scoop, scoop about 2 tablespoons Yellow Cake Pop Base. Form into a mouse head. Place on the prepared baking sheet. Repeat the process with the remaining cake pop base. Cover the baking sheet with plastic wrap and refrigerate for 30 minutes.

Step One
Melt the candy coating wafers in a bowl over simmering water or in the microwave on the defrost setting. Remove from the heat and let cool for 5 minutes. Meanwhile, remove the cake pops from the refrigerator and let rest for 5 minutes. Dip each lollipop stick about 1 inch (2.5 cm) deep in the melted candy coating, then insert it in the bottom of each cake pop. Place each cake pop, stick up, on the baking sheet. Set aside for 15 minutes at room temperature. Keep the candy coating warm.

Step Two
Once the candy coating has secured the stick, dip and swirl each cake pop in the warm candy coating. Insert the lollipop sticks in a block of Styrofoam. Set aside in a cool place, not the refrigerator, for about 30 minutes.

Step Three
Roll out the pale pink fondant to ⅛-inch (3-mm) thickness. Using a paring knife, cut 2 x 1-inch (2.5-cm) ears for each pop and attach with edible glue. Pinch off small pieces of dark pink fondant and roll each into a nose for each pop. Attach with edible glue or melted candy coating. Then attach white sugar pearls for eyes. With the melted cocoa butter mixed with black dusting powder, paint on the pupils of the eyes as well as the eyebrows. Place upright in the Styrofoam block. Will keep for up to 3 days at room temperature.

Pink Piglet

Make a farmyard animal themed pop display with the cute little animals featured here and over the next several pages.

POP BASE INGREDIENTS
Yellow Cake Base, page 20

DECORATING INGREDIENTS
8 oz. (½ bag) pink candy coating wafers
Paper lollipop sticks
4 oz. fondant, tinted pink
2 oz. fondant, tinted black

TO MAKE THE PINK PIGLET POPS
Line a baking sheet with baking parchment. Using an ice cream scoop, scoop about 2 tablespoons Yellow Cake Pop Base. Roll into a ball and place on the prepared baking sheet. Repeat the process with the remaining cake pop base. Cover the ball shapes with plastic wrap and refrigerate for 30 minutes.

Step One
Melt the candy coating wafers in a bowl over simmering water or in the microwave on the defrost setting. Remove from the heat and let cool for 5 minutes. Meanwhile, remove the cake pops from the refrigerator and let rest for 5 minutes. Dip each lollipop stick about 1 inch (2.5 cm) deep in the melted candy coating, then insert it in the bottom of each cake pop. Place each cake pop, stick up, on the baking sheet. Set aside for 15 minutes at room temperature. Keep the candy coating warm.

Step Two
Roll out the pink fondant to ⅛-inch (3-mm) thickness and with a round cutter cut out circles about ½ inch (1.25 cm) in diameter. Pinch the bottom half of the circle and taper the top with your fingers to form pigs' ears. Cut off the bottom with a knife to create a flat surface area. Repeat with all the ears and set to one side. To make the tails, pinch off a piece of pink fondant and roll into a long thin tube. Twist around a toothpick and let harden.

Step Three
Once the candy coating has secured the lollipop sticks, dip and swirl each cake pop in the warm candy coating. While the candy coating is still wet, attach the ears to the cake pop. Insert each lollipop stick in a Styrofoam block. Set aside in a cool place, not the refrigerator, for about 30 minutes while the coating sets. Keep the rest of the candy coating warm. Pinch off pieces of pink fondant and create flattened balls to form the snouts. Use a toothpick to create nostrils. Pinch off pieces of black fondant and roll into tiny balls to form the eyes. Attach the snouts, eyes, and tails with the warm candy coating. Place upright in the Styrofoam block. Will keep for up to 3 days at room temperature or 1 week in an airtight container in the fridge.

Yellow cake cute cow, see page 90

Cute Cow

Give the cow some black markings by attaching some rolled fondant, tinted black, with edible glue in a pattern of your choice.

POP BASE INGREDIENTS
Yellow Cake Base, page 20

DECORATING INGREDIENTS
8 oz. (½ bag) white candy coating wafers
Paper lollipop sticks
4 oz. fondant, tinted black
2 oz. fondant, tinted pink
White chocolate chips

TO MAKE THE CUTE COW POPS
Line a baking sheet with baking parchment. Using an ice cream scoop, scoop about 2 tablespoons Yellow Cake Pop Base. Roll into a ball and place on the prepared baking sheet. Repeat the process with the remaining cake pop base. Cover the ball shapes with plastic wrap and refrigerate for 30 minutes.

Step One
Melt the candy coating wafers in a bowl over simmering water or in the microwave on the defrost setting. Remove from the heat and let cool for 5 minutes. Meanwhile, remove the cake pops from the refrigerator and let rest for 5 minutes. Dip each lollipop stick about 1 inch (2.5 cm) deep in the melted candy

coating, then insert it in the bottom of each cake pop. Place each cake pop, stick up, on the baking sheet. Set aside for 15 minutes at room temperature. Keep the candy coating warm.

Step Two
Roll out the black fondant to ⅛-inch (3-mm) thickness and, with a small cutter, cut out circles ½ inch (1.25 cm) in diameter. Pinch the bottom half of the circle to form the cow's ears. Cut the bottom off with a knife to create a flat surface area. Repeat with all the ears and set to one side. Pinch off pieces of pink fondant and make tiny balls, flatten, and attach to the inside of the ears with a dab of warm candy coating. Create the cow's nose by pinching off pieces of pink fondant, and forming into a flat oval shape. Make 2 holes with a toothpick and attach tiny balls of pink fondant with warm candy coating.

Step Three
Once the candy coating has secured the lollipop sticks, dip and swirl each cake pop in the warm candy coating. While the candy coating is still wet, attach the ears and nose to the cake pop. Insert each lollipop stick in a Styrofoam block. Set aside in a cool place, not the refrigerator, for about 30 minutes while the coating sets. Keep the rest of the candy coating warm. Pinch off pieces of black fondant and roll into tiny balls to form the eyes. Attach the eyes with the warm candy coating. Attach the white chocolate chips with warm candy coating to create the horns. Place upright in the Styrofoam block. Will keep for up to 3 days at room temperature or 1 week in an airtight container in the fridge.

Funny Bunny

Peter Cottontail is hopping down the bunny trail, with a brief stop at the marshmallow patch.

POP BASE INGREDIENTS

2 cups confectioners' sugar, plus more for dusting
Coconut Marshmallow Base, page 25 (made in silicone half-sphere molds and an 8-inch (20-cm) silicone baking pan)

DECORATING INGREDIENTS

6 oz. white chocolate chips
Paper lollipop sticks
1 oz. fondant, tinted black
1 oz. white fondant
Edible pink dusting powder

TO MAKE THE FUNNY BUNNY POPS

Sift the confectioners' sugar onto a work surface. Invert the firm marshmallow base and the half sphere shapes onto the prepared surface; remove any parchment.

Step One

Melt the white chocolate in a bowl over simmering water or in the microwave using the defrost setting. Glue together the marshmallow half spheres with the melted white chocolate, sandwiching a lollipop stick between them. Let bunny heads set in a block of Styrofoam for 10 minutes. Keep the white chocolate warm.

Step Two

Using a paring knife heated in a mug of hot water, cut out 24 x 1-inch (2.5-cm) long ears and 12 x ½-inch (1.25-cm) wide round noses from the square marshmallow shape. Dust lightly with confectioners' sugar. Attach the ears and nose to each bunny head with melted white chocolate. Insert the pops in the Styrofoam block to dry for 10 minutes. Keep the chocolate warm.

Step Three

Pinch off small pieces of black fondant and form the eyes. Attach eyes to each bunny head with melted white chocolate. Pinch off small pieces of white fondant and form a row of front teeth. Score lines for individual teeth with a knife. Attach teeth with melted white chocolate. With a dry brush, brush the pink dusting powder onto the ears. Let the pops dry in the Styrofoam block in a cool place for 15 minutes. The pops will keep for 1 day in a cool, dry place (the fondant prevents them from being put in plastic to keep for longer—the fondant will absorb the moisture from the marshmallow and melt).

Sheep

After making these sheep pops, create a special grassy spot for them to "graze." Tint sweetened flaked coconut green and attach it to the Styrofoam block with edible glue or melted white chocolate.

POP BASE INGREDIENTS
Meringue Base, page 22

DECORATING INGREDIENTS
6 oz. white chocolate chips
Edible black pen
Black sugar pearls
Paper lollipop sticks

TO MAKE THE SHEEP MERINGUE POPS

Preheat the oven to 200°F (95°C). Line 2 large baking sheets with silicone baking liners or baking parchment. Spoon half the meringue mixture into a piping bag fitted with a round tip. Spoon the other half into a piping bag fitted with an open star tip. Using the first piping bag, pipe the meringue onto the prepared baking sheets in 2-inch (5-cm) long blobs (spaced 1 inch (2.5 cm) apart), dipping the tip down at the end of each blob and raising it up quickly to form a sheep's head and horns. Repeat until you have used all the meringue in that bag. With the open star-tipped piping bag, pipe a woolly coat onto each sheep's head. Bake for 3 hours or until the meringues are dry and can be easily removed from the baking sheets. Cool completely on wire racks in a dry room.

Step One
Melt the white chocolate chips in a bowl over simmering water or in the microwave on the defrost setting.

Step Two
Attach black sugar pearls as eyes to the meringue with the melted chocolate. Draw on a face with the edible black pen.

Step Three
Attach a lollipop stick in the center of each sheep with the melted chocolate. Set aside to dry in a cool place. Set in a Styrofoam block to dry for 15 minutes. Will keep at dry room temperature for 2 days.

Coconut marshmallow funny bunny, see page 91

Gnomes

Their jaunty red caps and curious expressions make these little treats fun for the holidays. If you like, pair them with the Woodland Mushroom Pops (page 117).

POP BASE INGREDIENTS
Meringue Base, page 22

DECORATING INGREDIENTS
1 cup (6 oz.) white chocolate chips
Chocolate red food coloring (or red candy melts)
Edible black pen
Paper lollipop sticks
White fondant

TO MAKE THE GNOME POPS
Preheat the oven to 200°F (95°C). Line 2 large baking sheets with silicone baking liners or parchment paper. Spoon meringue mixture into a piping bag fitted with a round tip. Pipe the meringue onto the prepared baking sheets in 2-inch (5-cm) wide blobs (spaced 1 inch (2.5 cm) apart), dipping the tip down into each blob and raising it up quickly to form a peak. Repeat until you have used all the meringue. Bake for 3 hours or until the meringues are dry and can be easily removed from the baking sheets. Cool completely on wire racks in a dry room.

Step One
Melt the white chocolate in a bowl over simmering water or in the microwave on the defrost setting. When the chocolate has melted, tint it with chocolate red food coloring and stir until smooth.

Step Two
Dip a lollipop stick in the melted red chocolate and insert it in the center of each gnome. Insert sticks in a Styrofoam block and set aside for 15 minutes in a dry place. Keep the chocolate warm.

Step Three
Turn each gnome upside down and dip the tip into the warm red chocolate to form a cap. Draw eyes with the edible black pen. Pinch off pieces of white fondant and make mustaches. Attach to the meringue with warm chocolate. Insert sticks in the Styrofoam block in a dry place to set for 15 minutes. Will keep at dry room temperature for 2 days and in an airtight container for 1 week.

Wedding Cake

As favors for a bridesmaids' luncheon or a bridal shower, these pops are tops.

POP BASE INGREDIENTS
Vegetable oil
Double Chocolate Brownie Base, page 27

DECORATING INGREDIENTS
1 (16-oz.) bag white candy coating wafers (more if necessary)
Paper lollipop sticks
2 oz. gum paste, tinted black

TO MAKE THE WEDDING CAKE POPS
Preheat the oven to 300°F (150°C). Brush each brownie mold cup with oil. Carefully spoon in the brownie batter so that each prepared cup is two-thirds full. (If you have only 1 brownie pop pan, do this in batches.) Bake for 20–25 minutes or until the brownies start to pull away from the sides of each cup. Carefully loosen brownies from the cups and turn out onto wire racks to cool completely.

Step One
Cut ½ inch (1.25 cm) off the top of each brownie and discard. Cut the remaining brownie in half horizontally. Keep the bottom halves together on a work surface; turn the top halves upside down and set aside.

Step Two
Melt the white candy coating wafers in a bowl over simmering water or in the microwave on the defrost setting. Remove from the heat. Attach the 2 brownie layers with some warm candy coating. Set aside for 5 minutes. Dip each lollipop stick into the candy coating and insert into the bottom of each pop. Set aside for 5 minutes. Dip and swirl each brownie pop in the melted candy and place in a Styrofoam block. Let cool for 15 minutes. Keep candy coating warm.

Step Three
Roll out the black gum paste and cut out thin strips to wrap around the 2 "cake" layers and to make bow ribbons. Using a heart cutter and a round cutter, cut out small hearts and bow centers. Attach the black gum paste bands to the pop with warm candy coating. Assemble the bow with the candy coating and when it is set, attach it to the top of the pop. Place each pop in the Styrofoam block and let dry. Brownie pops will keep in a plastic container for up to 3 days.

Brownie | 15 mins | makes 16-20

Sand Castle

Take these on a beach picnic or for a weekend jaunt to a favorite seaside cottage. Making these is also a great rainy day activity for kids when making real sand castles outside is not possible.

POP BASE INGREDIENTS
Vegetable oil
Rocky Road Brownie Base,
    page 27

DECORATING INGREDIENTS
Paper lollipop sticks
1 lb. (1 bag) yellow candy coating
    wafers (more if necessary)
White fondant, tinted brown
Edible glue
Yellow sanding sugar
Unfurled flag cupcake toppers (on
    a stick) or 24 toothpicks and
    red gum paste

HOW TO MAKE THE SAND CASTLE BROWNIE POPS
Preheat the oven to 300°F (150°C). Brush each brownie mold cup with oil. Carefully spoon in the brownie batter so that each prepared cup is two-thirds full. (If you have only one brownie pop pan, do this in batches.) Bake for 20–25 minutes or until the brownies start to pull away from the sides of each cup. Carefully loosen brownies from the cups and turn out onto wire racks to cool completely.

Step One
Cut ¼ inch (6.5 mm) off the top and bottom of each brownie and discard. With a knife, cut out 2 strips from the top of the "castle" to leave turrets. Melt the yellow candy coating wafers in a bowl over simmering water or in the microwave on the defrost setting. Remove from the heat. Dip a lollipop stick into the melted candy and insert into the bottom of a pop. Set aside, upside down, on a work surface to cool for 15 minutes. Repeat the process with all the pops. Keep the melted candy coating warm.

Step Two
Dip and swirl each brownie pop in the melted candy coating, then insert the lollipop sticks in a Styrofoam block. Let cool for 15 minutes.

Step Three
Roll out the brown fondant and cut out the doors. Attach to the pop with melted candy coating. Paint over the pop and the edge of the doors with edible glue and sprinkle on the yellow sugar. Gently shake off any excess. Insert a flag cupcake topper (or make your own flag from rolled gum paste attached to half a toothpick with candy coating and let dry). Repeat until all the pops are made and have dried for 15 minutes. Brownie pops will keep in a plastic container for up to 3 days.

Spring Tulip

Rocky Road brownie tulips—an exotic, new variety! Tie a green ribbon at the base of each pop to suggest leaves.

POP BASE INGREDIENTS

Vegetable oil
Rocky Road Brownie Base,
 page 27

DECORATING INGREDIENTS

Paper lollipop sticks
8 oz. (½ bag) red candy coating
 wafers (more if necessary)
2 oz. green gum paste
Green ribbon

HOW TO MAKE THE SPRING TULIP POPS

Preheat the oven to 300°F (150°C). Brush each brownie mold cup with vegetable oil. Carefully spoon in the brownie batter so that each prepared cup is two-thirds full. (If you have only one brownie pop pan, do this in batches.) Bake for 20–25 minutes or until the brownies start to pull away from the sides of each cup. Carefully loosen from the pan and turn out onto wire racks to cool completely.

Step One

Cut off the rough bottom of each brownie and round off the edges by trimming around the base. Cut 2 triangles out of the top of each brownie to form a tulip shape.

Step Two

Melt the red candy coating wafers in a bowl over simmering water or in the microwave on the defrost setting. Remove from the heat. Dip a lollipop stick into the warm candy coating and stick it into the bottom of the "tulip." Set aside for 5 minutes. Repeat with each brownie. Dip and swirl each brownie pop in the melted coating and place in a Styrofoam block to cool for 15 minutes.

Step Three

Roll out the green gum paste and cut out leaves using a flower cutter. Attach with melted candy coating to the base of the tulip. Let cool completely, then tie green ribbon on each pop to suggest tulip leaves. Brownie pops will keep in a plastic container for up to 3 days.

Wizard Wand

Straight from the wizard's kitchen, these crunchy treats will cast a sweet spell. Make sure to pour the honeycomb candy while it's still hot. You'll need two star-shaped cookie pop pans for this recipe.

POP BASE INGREDIENTS
Vegetable oil
Paper lollipop sticks
Honeycomb Candy Base,
**   page 23**

DECORATING INGREDIENTS
4 oz. fondant, tinted purple
4 oz. fondant, tinted yellow
Edible glue
Thin red or multicolored ribbon

TO MAKE THE WIZARD WAND POPS
Brush the inside of each star-shaped cookie mold with oil. Place the lollipop sticks so that they reach to the center of each mold. Carefully and evenly pour the hot honeycomb into the prepared pan so that the lollipop sticks are fully covered. Let cool completely in a dry room.

Step One
Remove from the molds. Roll out the purple fondant to ¼-inch (6.5-mm) thickness and cut out medium stars. Roll out the yellow fondant to ¼-inch (6.5-mm) thickness and cut out small stars. Attach the small star to the medium star with edible glue, and then attach to the center of each candy pop with the glue.

Step Two
Tie thin, trailing ribbon at the base of each star. Set pops in a block of Styrofoam to dry in a dry place. Will keep for 1 day at dry room temperature.

103

Honeycomb · 10 mins · makes 8

Sweet Blossom

These easy pink blossom pops make a great weekend or sleepover "keep-the-kids-busy" project. To make them, you'll need blossom-shaped cookie pop pans.

POP BASE INGREDIENTS
Vegetable oil
Paper lollipop sticks
Honeycomb Candy Base,
    page 23

DECORATING INGREDIENTS
4 oz. fondant, tinted yellow
8 oz. (½ bag) pink candy coating
    wafers

TO MAKE THE SWEET BLOSSOM HONEYCOMB POPS

Brush the inside of each cookie pop mold with oil. Place the lollipop sticks so that they reach to the center of each mold. Carefully and evenly pour the hot honeycomb into the prepared pan so that the lollipop sticks are fully covered. Let cool completely in a dry room.

Step One
Remove the blossoms from the molds. Roll out the yellow fondant to ¼-inch (6.5-mm) thickness and cut out circles with a round cutter. Melt the pink candy coating wafers in a bowl over simmering water or in the microwave on the defrost setting. Remove from the heat. Attach the circles to the middle of each flower with the candy coating. Brush or pipe on the melted candy to form the petals of each blossom.

Step Two
Set pops upright in a block of Styrofoam to dry in a dry place. Will keep for 3 days at dry room temperature and in an airtight container for 1 week.

Christmas Tree

After making the pops in two Christmas tree-shaped cookie pop pans, decorate them with sugar garlands.

POP BASE INGREDIENTS
Vegetable oil
Paper lollipop sticks
Honeycomb Candy Base,
    page 23

DECORATING INGREDIENTS
8 oz. (½ bag) red candy coating
    wafers
Gold sugar pearls
4 oz. gum paste, tinted yellow

TO MAKE THE CHRISTMAS TREE POPS
Brush the inside of each Christmas tree-shaped cookie pop mold with oil. Place the lollipop sticks so that they reach to the center of each mold. Carefully and evenly pour the hot honeycomb candy into the oiled molds so that the lollipop sticks are fully covered. Let cool completely in a dry room.

Step One
Remove from the molds. Melt the red candy coating wafers in a bowl over simmering water or in the microwave on the defrost setting. Remove from the heat. Brush or pipe on the melted candy to form the garlands on each tree.

Step Two
Place the gold sugar pearls on the peaks of the garlands. Roll out the yellow gum paste to ¼-inch (6.5-mm) thickness and cut out stars with a cutter. Attach to the top of each tree with the melted candy coating. Set upright in a Styrofoam block to dry in a dry place. Will keep at dry room temperature for 1 day and in an airtight container for 1 week.

Wedding Bells

With this recipe, you can make wedding bells, school bells, or bells to ring in the holidays. Simply customize the chocolate or candy coating and type of decorations to suit the occasion. Make sure the white chocolate coating is generous, so the dark brownie does not show through.

POP BASE INGREDIENTS
Chocolate Brownie Base, page 27
Paper lollipop sticks

DECORATING INGREDIENTS
1 cup (6 oz.) white chocolate chips, plus more if necessary
4 oz. white fondant
Edible glue
4 oz. gum paste
Edible silver paint

HOW TO MAKE THE WEDDING BELL POPS
Preheat the oven to 300°F (150°C). Brush each brownie mold cup with oil. Carefully spoon in the brownie batter so that each prepared cup is two-thirds full. (If you have only one brownie pop pan, do this in batches.) Bake for 15 minutes, remove from the oven, and insert a lollipop stick in the center of each brownie. Return to the oven and bake for 5–10 more minutes or until the brownies start to pull away from the sides of each cup. Carefully loosen from the pan and turn out onto wire racks to cool completely.

Step One
Melt the white chocolate chips in a bowl over simmering water or in the microwave on the defrost setting. Remove from the heat. Dip and swirl each brownie pop in the melted chocolate, then place them in a block of Styrofoam to cool for 15 minutes.

Step Two
Pinch off pieces of white fondant and roll small cylinders for each pop to form the handle. Attach with edible glue or white chocolate. Roll out the gum paste to $\frac{1}{16}$-inch (3-mm) thickness. Cut it into strips, $\frac{1}{4}$ inch (6.5 mm) wide by 1 inch (2.5 cm) long, to form a small bow for each brownie pop. Also, cut strips $\frac{3}{16}$ inch (5 mm) thick and long enough to wrap around the base of the bell. Attach with edible glue or white chocolate. With edible silver paint, brush on polka-dot or damask designs.

Step Three
Let pops cool completely in the block of Styrofoam for 15 minutes. Brownie pops will keep in a plastic container for up to 3 days.

Clown

Use your imagination or artistic license and create a circus full of clown pops. Make them all the same or individualize each one.

POP BASE INGREDIENTS
Yellow Cake Base, page 20

DECORATING INGREDIENTS
8 oz. (½ bag) skin tone or pink candy coating wafers (more if necessary)
Paper lollipop sticks
4 oz. fondant, tinted red
Edible glue
1 oz. white gum paste
1 oz. gum paste, tinted purple
Cocoa butter, melted
Edible black dusting powder

TO MAKE THE CLOWN POPS
Line a baking sheet with parchment paper. With an ice cream scoop, scoop about 2 tablespoons Yellow Cake Pop Base. Form into a ball. Place on the prepared baking sheet. Repeat the process with the remaining cake pop base. Cover the baking sheet with plastic wrap and refrigerate for 30 minutes.

Step One
Melt the candy coating wafers in a bowl over simmering water or in the microwave on the defrost setting. Remove from the heat and let cool for 5 minutes. Meanwhile, remove the cake pops from the refrigerator and let rest for 5 minutes. Dip each lollipop stick about 1 inch (2.5 cm) deep in the melted candy coating, then insert it in the bottom of each cake pop. Place each cake pop, stick up, on the baking sheet. Set aside for 15 minutes at room temperature. Keep the candy coating warm.

Step Two
Once the candy coating has secured the stick, dip and swirl each cake pop in the warm candy coating. Insert the lollipop sticks in a block of Styrofoam. Set aside in a cool place, not the refrigerator, for about 30 minutes.

Step Three
Roll out the red fondant to ⅛-inch (3-mm) thickness. Using a 1-inch (2.5-cm) wide flower cutter, cut 2 flowers for each pop. Gather up the scraps, pinch off small pieces, and roll each into a nose for each pop. Attach the flower "hair" and nose with edible glue or the melted candy coating. Pinch off small pieces of white gum paste and form 2 oval eyeballs for each pop. Pinch off small pieces of purple gum paste and form 2 eyebrows for each pop. Attach all parts with edible glue or melted candy coating. With melted cocoa butter mixed with edible black dusting powder, paint on the pupils. Place upright in the Styrofoam block. Will keep for up to 3 days at room temperature, but it is best to store in the refrigerator in an airtight container.

Cheshire Cat

Like these pops, the Cheshire cat appears—and then disappears—except for the toothy smile. You will need 2 round cookie pop pans for this recipe or heat the toffee in 2 batches.

POP BASE INGREDIENTS

Vegetable oil
Paper lollipop sticks
Chewy Orange Toffee Base,
     page 29

DECORATING INGREDIENTS

4 oz. orange candy coating wafers
4 oz. white fondant
4 oz. white fondant, tinted pink
4 oz. white fondant, tinted black
4 oz. white fondant, tinted dark
     brown
Cocoa butter, melted
Edible black dusting powder

TO MAKE THE CHESHIRE CAT POPS

Brush the inside of each round cookie pop mold with oil. Place the lollipop sticks so that they reach to the center of each mold. Carefully divide the hot toffee among the prepared molds so that the lollipop sticks are fully covered. Let cool completely.

Top Pop Tip

Use a spare lollipop stick for the ears to rest on while they harden to the toffee.

Step One

Remove from the molds. Melt the orange candy coating wafers in a bowl over simmering water or in the microwave on the defrost setting. Remove from the heat. Using a fine paintbrush or a piping bag fitted with a small round tip, apply the melted candy onto each pop to make the cat's facial stripes. Roll out the white fondant and cut out big toothy smiles with a knife. Attach with warm candy coating. Create eyes with the white fondant and pupils with the black fondant. Pinch off pieces of brown fondant to create the ears and use small pieces of pink fondant to make the inner ear. Attach ears to cats with warm candy coating. Pinch off a piece of pink fondant, shape it into a nose, and attach with warm candy coating. Finally, using melted cocoa butter mixed with black dusting powder, paint lines to create the teeth.

Step Two

Set the pops upright in a Styrofoam block to dry in a dry (not humid) place for 15 minutes. Will keep in an airtight container in a cool, dry place (not the refrigerator) for up to 1 week.

Bee Blossom

Bees aren't the only ones who find these cookie pops irresistible!

POP BASE INGREDIENTS

**Almond Spritz Cookie Base,
    page 26**

DECORATING INGREDIENTS

**1 recipe Cookie Frosting
    (page 26), tinted blue**
**½ recipe Cookie Frosting
    (page 26), tinted yellow**
Yellow sanding sugar
Paper lollipop sticks
4 oz. fondant, tinted yellow
2 oz. fondant, tinted black

White sugar pearls
Cocoa butter, melted
Edible black dusting powder
½ cup sliced almonds
Edible glue

TO MAKE THE BEE BLOSSOM POPS

Preheat the oven to 400°F (200°C). On a lightly floured work surface, roll out the dough to ¼- to ½-inch (6.5- to 13-mm) thickness. Cut into shapes with a flower cookie cutter. Place cookies 1 inch (2.5 cm) apart on ungreased baking sheets. Bake for 10–12 minutes or until lightly browned at the edges. Transfer cookies to wire racks and cool completely.

Step One

Pour half the blue frosting into a piping bag with a size 2 round tip. Outline the petals on each cooled cookie with the blue frosting, then fill in the rest. Refill the piping bag with the remaining blue frosting as necessary. Let dry (about 8 hours).

Step Two

Pour the yellow frosting into a piping bag with a size 2 round tip. Outline the center of the flower on each cookie with the frosting, and then fill in the center. While the yellow frosting is still moist, sprinkle yellow sanding sugar onto the yellow centers of each cookie. Let the cookies dry for 3 hours. Then attach the lollipop stick to the back of the cookie with some frosting. Let dry upside down, for 8 hours or overnight.

Step Three

Pinch off small pieces of yellow fondant and form a tiny bee's body. Create stripes on the body with black fondant. Attach white sugar pearls for eyes and brush on pupils made by mixing melted cocoa butter with a little black dusting powder. Attach almond slices to each body with edible glue to make wings, then attach the bee to the cookie with frosting. Place cookie pops flat on a baking sheet. Will keep in an airtight container for 1 week.

Mocha meringue egg's nest, see page 116; meringue woodland mushroom, see page 117

Egg's Nest

For springtime or for someone feathering a new nest, make these meringue treats with pastel chocolate eggs.

POP BASE INGREDIENTS

Mocha Meringue Base, page 22

DECORATING INGREDIENTS

1 cup (6 oz.) white chocolate chips
2 milk chocolate bars
Pastel candy-coated miniature chocolate eggs
Paper lollipop sticks

TO MAKE THE EGG'S NEST POPS

Preheat the oven to 200°F (95°C). Line 2 large baking sheets with silicone baking liners or parchment paper. Spoon the meringue into a piping bag fitted with an open star tip. In a spiral motion, pipe the base and then the walls of a bird's nest onto the prepared baking sheets into 2-inch (5-cm) wide circles, spaced 1 inch (2.5 cm) apart. Using a toothpick, rough up the walls of the nest. Bake for 4 hours or until the meringues are dry and can be easily removed from the baking sheets. Cool completely on wire racks in a dry room.

Step One

Melt the white chocolate in a bowl over simmering water or in the microwave on the defrost setting. Brush the bottom of each nest with melted white chocolate. Keep the white chocolate warm. Using a vegetable peeler, shave milk chocolate into the well of each nest.

Step Two

Dip the bottom of each candy egg in white chocolate and attach to the nest. Let dry on a flat surface for 15 minutes, while still keeping the white chocolate warm.

Step Three

Attach a lollipop stick to the bottom of each nest with the melted chocolate. Insert in a Styrofoam block in a dry place to dry for 15 minutes. Will keep in an airtight container for 1 week.

Meringue · 5 mins · makes 24-36

Woodland Mushroom

Dusted with a little cocoa powder, these pops look like the real thing.

POP BASE INGREDIENTS
Meringue Base, page 22

DECORATING INGREDIENTS
1 cup (6 oz.) semisweet chocolate chips
Paper lollipop sticks
Cocoa powder

TO MAKE THE WOODLAND MUSHROOM POPS
Preheat the oven to 200°F (95°C). Line 2 large baking sheets with silicone baking liners or parchment paper. Place meringue in a piping bag fitted with a large round tip. Onto one of the prepared baking sheets, pipe 1-inch (2.5-cm) wide blobs (spacing them 1 inch (2.5 cm) apart). Dab the top down with a wet finger to create a smooth, rounded finish. These will be the tops of the mushrooms. With the remaining meringue, pipe 1-inch (2.5-cm) lengths (spaced 1 inch (2.5 cm) apart) onto the second baking sheet, then dip the tip downward and up to create a blunt end for the mushroom stem. Bake both sheets for 4 hours or until the meringues are dry and can be easily removed from the pan. Cool completely on wire racks in a dry room.

Top Pop Tip
Dab the top of the uncooked meringue with a wet finger to create a smooth finish.

Step One
Melt the chocolate chips in a bowl over simmering water or in the microwave on the defrost setting. Keep the chocolate warm.

Step Two
Dip the bottom of each mushroom cap and the tip of each mushroom stem in the chocolate and put them together to make a mushroom. Place them upside down or on their sides on the baking sheet to dry for 15 minutes.

Step Three
Gently insert a lollipop stick in the center of each mushroom stem with melted chocolate. Dust with cocoa powder. Set in a Styrofoam block to dry in a dry place. Will keep in an airtight container for 1 week.

Shooting Star

Popping candy sends these cookie treats into another dimension when you take a bite.

POP BASE INGREDIENTS
Fresh Lime or Sugar 'n' Spice Cookie Base, page 26

DECORATING INGREDIENTS
Cookie Frosting (page 26), tinted yellow
Popping candy
2 oz. white fondant
Edible glue
Paper lollipop sticks

TO MAKE THE SHOOTING STAR POPS
Preheat the oven to 400°F (200°C). On a lightly floured work surface, roll out the dough to ¼- to ½-inch (6.5- to 13-mm) thickness. Cut into shapes with a shooting star cookie cutter. Place cookies 1 inch (2.5 cm) apart on ungreased cookie sheets. Bake for 10–12 minutes or until lightly browned at the edges. Transfer cookies to wire racks and cool completely.

Step One
Pour half the yellow frosting into a piping bag fitted with a size 2 round tip. Outline the shooting star with the frosting, then fill in the rest. Sprinkle with popping candy while the frosting is still moist. Repeat the process until all the cookies are frosted and decorated.

Step Two
Let the cookies dry for 8 hours on wire racks. Roll out the white fondant to $\frac{1}{8}$-inch (3-mm) thickness. With a star cookie cutter or a paring knife, cut out stars. Attach to the cookie with edible glue.

Step Three
Attach a lollipop stick to the back of the cookie with frosting. Let dry, then place upright in a Styrofoam block. Will keep in an airtight container for 1 week.

Tick Tock

You can personalize these cookie pops, if you wish, by drawing the hands of the clock to a memorable hour and minute. Unless you have several round cookie pop pans, allow a little extra time to bake these.

POP BASE INGREDIENTS

Vegetable oil
Sugar 'n' Spice Cookie Base, page 26
Paper lollipop sticks

DECORATING INGREDIENTS

2 oz. white fondant
Edible glue
2 oz. black candy coating wafers
2 oz. fondant, tinted black

TO MAKE THE TICK TOCK POPS

Preheat the oven to 400°F (200°C). Brush the inside of the cookie pop pan with oil. Pinch off 6 pieces of dough, flatten slightly on a floured surface, and press into each cookie pop mold. Fill each mold up to ⅛ inch (3 mm) from the top edge. Gently slide in each lollipop stick to reach the middle of the mold. Bake for 12–14 minutes, or until lightly browned at the edges. Let cool in the pan for 30 minutes, then carefully invert cookies onto wire racks to cool completely. Repeat the process with the remaining dough.

Top Pop Tip

Practice piping on a piece of baking paper before you attempt this cookie pop.

Step One

When the cookies are cool, roll out the white fondant to ⅛-inch (3-mm) thickness. With a round cookie cutter, cut out a circle about ³⁄₁₆ inch (5 mm) less in diameter than the cookie. Attach the circle to the cookie with edible glue.

Step Two

Melt the candy coating wafers in a bowl over simmering water or in the microwave on the defrost setting. Pour the warm candy coating into a piping bag fitted with a size 2 round tip. Write the numbers for the hours (12, 3, 6, and 9) around the face of the clock and the dots for the hours between. Set the cookies aside for 30 minutes to dry. Roll out the black fondant to ⅛-inch (3-mm) thickness and, with a paring knife, cut out the hour and minute hands of each clock. With round cutters, cut out the two circles for the clock hands and attach to each other with edible glue. Attach the hands to each clock face with edible glue.

Step Three

When the clock faces have dried, set the cookies upright in a Styrofoam block. Will keep in an airtight container for 1 week.

Chapter 4

Butter Brittle · 20 mins · makes 8

Ship's Wheel

Steer a sweet course through life's choppy waters with these ship's wheel pops. You'll need two round cookie pop pans to make these pops, or heat the brittle in two batches.

POP BASE INGREDIENTS
Vegetable oil
Paper lollipop sticks
Butter Brittle Base, page 28

DECORATING INGREDIENTS
8 oz. brown candy coating wafers
8 oz. fondant, tinted light brown

Brown sugar-coated chocolate button (a large smartie or M&M)
Chocolate "O"-shaped cereal
Chocolate sticks
White sugar pearls

TO MAKE THE SHIP'S WHEEL POPS
Brush the inside of each round cookie pop mold with oil. Place the lollipop sticks so that they reach to the center of each mold. Carefully divide the hot brittle candy among the prepared molds so that the lollipop sticks are fully covered. Let cool completely.

Step One
Remove from the molds. Melt the candy coating wafers in a bowl over simmering water or in the microwave on the defrost setting. Remove from the heat. Roll out the light brown fondant to 1/16-inch (1.5-mm) thickness and, with a round cutter, cut out the wheel for the pop. Attach to the brittle pops with candy coating. With more candy coating, attach a brown sugar-coated chocolate button to the middle of a chocolate "O"-shaped cereal, then attach it to the center of each pop. Cut off the ends of the chocolate sticks and attach them with candy coating to the wheel to create the spokes. With the melted candy coating, attach white sugar pearls around the wheel.

Step Two
Set the pops upright in a Styrofoam block to dry in a dry (not humid) place for 15 minutes. Will keep in an airtight container in a cool, dry place (not the refrigerator) for up to 1 week.

Brownie Ahoy, Mate! sailor, see page 82

St. Lucia Candle

A little cardamom in the sugar cookie dough—a traditional spice in Scandinavian baking—makes these cookie pops extra special. If you like, make a St. Lucia crown by standing these pops in a circle on a Styrofoam ring, surrounded by holiday greenery.

POP BASE INGREDIENTS

Cardamom Sugar Cookie Base,
  page 26

DECORATING INGREDIENTS

½ recipe white Cookie Frosting
  (page 26)
½ recipe Cookie Frosting
  (page 26), tinted red
½ recipe Cookie Frosting
  (page 26), tinted yellow
Paper lollipop sticks

TO MAKE THE ST. LUCIA CANDLE POPS

Preheat the oven to 400°F (200°C). On a lightly floured work surface, roll out the dough to ¼- to ½-inch (6.5- to 13-mm) thickness. Cut into shapes with a candle-shaped cookie cutter. Place cookies 1 inch (2.5 cm) apart on ungreased cookie sheets. Bake for 10–12 minutes or until lightly browned at the edges. Transfer to wire racks and cool completely.

Step One

Pour the white frosting into a piping bag fitted with a size 2 round tip. Outline the candle of each cookie with the white frosting, then fill in the rest of the candle.

Step Two

Pour the red frosting into a piping bag fitted with a size 2 round tip. Outline the bottom of each cookie candle with red frosting, then fill in the rest. Let the cookies dry for 1 hour. Pour the yellow frosting into a piping bag fitted with a size 2 round tip. Outline the candle flame with yellow frosting, then fill in the rest. Put a small dot of red frosting at the base of the flame and, with a toothpick, pull the dot upward to create an inner flame. Let the cookies dry for 1 hour.

Step Three

Attach a lollipop stick to the back of each cookie with frosting and stand upright in a Styrofoam block. Will keep in an airtight container for 1 week.

Starfish

For a poolside or beach party, create these sea-inspired treats.

POP BASE INGREDIENTS
Fresh Lime Sugar Cookie Base, page 26

DECORATING INGREDIENTS
Cookie Frosting (page 26), tinted orange
Large white sugar pearls
½ recipe white Cookie Frosting (page 26)
Paper lollipop sticks

TO MAKE THE STARFISH COOKIE POPS
Preheat the oven to 400°F (200°C). On a lightly floured work surface, roll out the dough to ¼- to ½-inch (6.5- to 13-mm) thickness. Cut into shapes with a starfish cookie cutter. Place cookies 1 inch (2.5 cm) apart on ungreased cookie sheets. Bake for 10–12 minutes or until lightly browned at the edges. Transfer to wire racks and cool completely.

Step One
Pour the orange frosting into a piping bag fitted with a size 2 round tip. Outline the perimeter of each starfish, then fill in the rest. Let the cookies dry for 2 hours. Attach sugar pearls to the starfish with the orange frosting.

Step Two
Pour the white frosting into a piping bag fitted with a size 2 round tip. Create the dots and other desired details on each starfish. Set aside for 2 hours or until dry.

Step Three
Attach a lollipop stick to the back of each cookie with frosting, let it set, then stand upright in a Styrofoam block. Will keep in an airtight container for 1 week.

Cookie · 40 mins · makes 24-30

Venetian Mask

The eyes have it in these mysterious cookie pops. Use just one color of hard candy or mix several colors for a stained-glass effect. To crush hard candies, place them between sheets of parchment paper and pound with a rolling pin.

POP BASE INGREDIENTS
Almond Spritz Sugar Cookie Base, page 26

DECORATING INGREDIENTS
½ cup crushed hard candies
½ recipe Cookie Frosting (page 26), tinted yellow (or more as needed)
Yellow edible glitter
½ recipe White Cookie Frosting (page 26), or more as needed
½ recipe Cookie Frosting (page 26), tinted purple (or more as needed)
2 oz. gum paste, tinted yellow
2 oz. gum paste, tinted pale purple
White sugar pearls or edible diamonds
Paper lollipop sticks

TO MAKE THE VENETIAN MASK POPS
Preheat the oven to 400°F (200°C). On a lightly floured work surface, roll out the dough to ¼- to ½-inch (6.5- to 13-mm) thickness. Cut into shapes with mask-shaped cookie cutter. Place cookies 1 inch (2.5 cm) apart on cookie sheets lined with silicone baking liners. Place ½ to 1 teaspoon crushed hard candy in each eye. Bake for 10–12 minutes or until the cookies have lightly browned at the edges and the candy has melted for the eyes. Let cool for 30 minutes, then carefully transfer to wire racks and cool completely.

Step One
Pour the yellow frosting into a piping bag fitted with a size 2 round tip. Outline the perimeter of each mask, the eyes, and extra details. Refill the bag as necessary. Sprinkle the yellow glitter onto the wet frosting. Let dry for a few hours. Shake off the excess glitter.

Step Two
Pour the white frosting into a piping bag fitted with a size 2 round tip. Fill in the lower sections on the mask. Pour the purple frosting into a piping bag and fill in the middle/upper section of the mask. Let dry for a few hours.

Step Three
Roll out the gum pastes to $\frac{1}{16}$-inch (1.5-mm) thickness and cut out tiny flowers with a flower cutter. Attach to the mask with frosting. Attach a sugar pearl or an edible diamond to the center of the flower with a dab of frosting. Attach a lollipop stick to the back of each cookie with frosting. Let dry for about 8 hours. Store flat until needed. Will keep in an airtight container for 1 week.

Surf's Up

For a fun beach treat, make these along with Starfish (page 126). Make sure to keep the meringue pops dry and away from humidity.

POP BASE INGREDIENTS

Tinted Meringue Pop Base, in ocean blue (page 22)

DECORATING INGREDIENTS

1 cup (6 oz.) white chocolate chips
Tiny white sugar pearls
Paper lollipop sticks

TO MAKE THE SURF'S UP POPS

Preheat the oven to 200°F (95°C). Line 2 large baking sheets with silicone baking liners or parchment paper. Fill a piping bag fitted with a large round tip with the meringue mixture. Pipe the meringue onto the prepared baking sheets in 2-inch (5-cm) wide blobs. Use the back of the spoon or a spatula to curl them up into a cresting wave. Place the meringues 1 inch (2.5 cm) apart. Bake for 4 hours or until the meringues are dry and can be easily removed from the baking sheets. Cool completely on wire racks in a dry room.

Top Pop Tip
Use the back of a wet spoon to smooth over the uncooked meringue.

Step One
Melt the white chocolate chips in a bowl over simmering water or in the microwave on the defrost setting.

Step Two
Turn each wave upside down and dip the tops in the melted chocolate. Attach sugar pearls for foam. Let dry on a flat surface for 15 minutes, while keeping the melted chocolate warm.

Step Three
Attach a lollipop stick in the center of each wave with melted chocolate. Insert in a Styrofoam block in a dry place to dry for 15 minutes. Will keep in an airtight container for 1 week.

Chewy Toffee   15 mins   makes 8-10

Tortoise

In a race with the fast-but-lazy hare, the slow-and-steady tortoise wins the day, according to *Aesop's Fables*. However, when you serve these pops, you can count on a race to get one before they're all gone. They are made in a mini-muffin pan.

POP BASE INGREDIENTS
Vegetable oil
Chewy Toffee Base, page 29
Paper lollipop sticks

DECORATING INGREDIENTS
4 oz. fondant, tinted green
2 oz. green candy coating wafers
White sugar pearls
Edible glue
Edible black dusting powder
Cocoa butter, melted

TO MAKE THE TORTOISE POPS
Brush the inside of the mini-muffin tray cups with oil. Carefully divide the hot toffee among the prepared cups. Let cool for 2 minutes, then insert the lollipop sticks so that they reach to the bottom center of each muffin cup and stay upright. Let them cool completely.

Step One
Remove the pops from the muffin cups and insert the lollipop sticks in a Styrofoam block.

Step Two
Pinch off pieces of green fondant and form each tortoise head, 4 legs, and a tail. Attach the fondant pieces to the pop with melted candy coating. Attach white sugar pearls for eyes with edible glue. Paint on black pupils with melted cocoa butter mixed with black dusting powder.

Step Three
Let pops dry in a dry place for 15 minutes. Will keep in a cool, dry place in an airtight container for up to 1 week.

Groovy Record

Play a vintage '33, '45, or '78 rpm record on a turntable and listen to that groovy music. You'll need two round cookie pop pans, or heat the brittle mixture in two batches.

POP BASE INGREDIENTS
Vegetable oil
Paper lollipop sticks
Butter Brittle with Almond,
    page 28

DECORATING INGREDIENTS
8 oz. (½ bag) white candy coating
    wafers
8 oz. fondant, tinted yellow
8 oz. fondant, tinted green
8 oz. fondant, tinted purple

TO MAKE THE GROOVY RECORD POPS
Brush the inside of 8 round cookie pop molds with oil. Place the lollipop sticks so that they reach to the center of each mold. Carefully divide the hot brittle candy among the prepared molds so that the lollipop sticks are fully covered. Let cool completely.

Step One
Remove the hardened pops from the molds. Melt the candy coating wafers in a bowl over simmering water or in the microwave on the defrost setting. Remove from the heat. Using a fine paintbrush or a piping bag fitted with a small round tip, brush or pipe the candy melt in a circular pattern to form the grooves in the record.

Step Two
Roll out the fondants to ⅛-inch (3-mm) thickness and, using small round cutters, cut out the centers for the records. Attach with the melted candy coating. Insert the pops in a Styrofoam block and let dry in a dry (not humid) place for 15 minutes. Will keep in a cool, dry place (not the refrigerator) for up to 1 week.

Chewy Toffee — 8 mins — makes 8-10

UFO

Unidentified flying objects—or irresistible treats? These pops are made in a mini-muffin pan.

POP BASE INGREDIENTS
Vegetable oil
Chewy Toffee Base, page 29
Paper lollipop sticks

DECORATING INGREDIENTS
2 oz. yellow candy coating wafers
Yellow sugar pearls
4 oz. white fondant
Edible silver spray

TO MAKE THE UFO POPS
Brush the inside of 16 mini-muffin cups with oil. Carefully divide the hot toffee among the prepared molds. Let cool 2 minutes, then insert the lollipop sticks so that they reach to the bottom center of each mold and stay upright. Let cool completely.

Step One
Remove the pops from the molds and insert the lollipop sticks in a Styrofoam block.

Step Two
Melt the candy coating wafers in a bowl over simmering water or in the microwave on the defrost setting. Remove from the heat. Attach yellow sugar pearls around the UFO with melted candy coating. Pinch off a piece of white fondant and shape a dome for the top of the UFO. Coat it with edible silver spray, and when it is dry attach to the top of the UFO with melted candy coating.

Step Three
Let dry in a dry place for 15 minutes. Will keep in an airtight container in a cool, dry place (not the refrigerator) for up to 1 week.

Yellow cake alien, see page 138; espresso bean truffle rings of Saturn, see page 139

Alien

These cake pops rocket to dessert stardom with a yellow, vanilla-flavored cake molded with a cream cheese frosting.

POP BASE INGREDIENTS
Yellow Cake Base, page 20

DECORATING INGREDIENTS
8 oz. (½ bag) white candy coating wafers (more if necessary)
Paper lollipop sticks
2 oz. gum paste, tinted green
2 oz. gum paste, tinted black
Edible glue or candy melt
1 oz. white fondant
Multicolored sugar pearls

TO MAKE THE ALIEN POPS
Line a baking sheet with parchment paper. Using an ice cream scoop, scoop about 2 tablespoons Yellow Cake Pop Base, then form into a ball. Place on the prepared baking sheet. Repeat the process with the remaining cake pop base. Cover the baking sheet with plastic wrap and refrigerate for 30 minutes.

Step One
Melt the candy coating wafers in a bowl over simmering water or in the microwave on the defrost setting. Remove from the heat and let cool for 5 minutes. Meanwhile, remove the cake pops from the refrigerator and let rest for 5 minutes. Dip each lollipop stick about 1 inch (2.5 cm) deep in the melted candy coating, then insert it in the bottom of each cake pop. Place each cake pop, stick up, on the baking sheet. Set aside for 15 minutes at room temperature. Keep the candy coating warm.

Step Two
Once the candy coating has secured the stick, dip and swirl each cake pop in the warm candy coating. Insert the lollipop sticks in a block of Styrofoam. Set aside in a cool place, not the refrigerator, for about 30 minutes.

Step Three
Roll out the green gum paste to ¹⁄₁₆-inch (1.5-mm) thickness. Using a small cookie cutter or paring knife, cut a 2-inch (5-cm) wide oval for the face of each alien. Attach to each pop with edible glue or candy melt. Roll out the white gum paste to ¹⁄₁₆-inch (1.5-mm) thickness. Using a paring knife, cut a 2-inch (5-cm) wide visor rim and attach to each pop with edible glue or candy melt. Roll out the black gum paste to ¹⁄₁₆-inch (1.5-mm) thickness and cut out ²⁄₃ x 2½-inch (1.75 x 7-cm) strips for the visor. Attach with candy melt. Roll out tiny balls of black gum paste and flatten to create the eyes. Attach with candy melt and attach button candies on each side of the helmet. Place upright in the Styrofoam block. Will keep for up to 3 days at room temperature.

Rings of Saturn

Make these out-of-this-world truffle pops and watch them disappear. They seem to emit a magnetic attraction toward just about anyone in the cosmos.

POP BASE INGREDIENTS
Espresso Bean Truffle Base, page 24

DECORATING INGREDIENTS
8 oz. (½ bag) orange candy coating wafers (more if necessary)
Paper lollipop sticks
2 oz. red candy melt
2 oz. blue candy melt
1 (0.85-oz.) package sugar sheets
Edible white glitter

TO MAKE THE RINGS OF SATURN POPS
Line a baking sheet with parchment paper. Remove the truffle mixture from the refrigerator. Using a small cookie scoop or large melon baller, scoop 24 (1-tablespoon-size) balls. Roll each into smooth balls and place on the prepared pan. Place in the refrigerator for 30 minutes.

Step One
Melt the orange candy coating wafers in a bowl over simmering water or in the microwave on the defrost setting. Remove from the heat.

Step Two
Remove the truffle pops from the refrigerator and insert a lollipop stick halfway into each. Dip and swirl each pop in the warm orange candy coating. Insert each lollipop stick in a block of Styrofoam and let dry for 15 minutes.

Step Three
Melt the blue and red candy melts in two different bowls over simmering water or in the microwave on the defrost setting. Remove from the heat. Add a little red and blue candy melt to the orange candy melt so that, when you dip the pop, a marbled effect is achieved. Cut out rings, with about a 1¾-inch (4-cm) diameter center and a ½-inch (13-mm) wide ring, from sugar sheets to fit over each truffle. Sprinkle the rings with edible white glitter. Paint with a little more melted candy coating to attach the rings to the pop. Set aside to dry in a cool place for 15 minutes. Will keep in an airtight container in the refrigerator for up to 3 days.

Chocolate Cake · 2 mins · makes 22-26

Bitten Cookie

Who stole the cookie from the cookie jar? Once you pop you won't stop.

POP BASE INGREDIENTS
Chocolate Cake Base, page 21

DECORATING INGREDIENTS
8 oz. (½ bag) peanut butter candy coating wafers
Paper lollipop sticks
Milk chocolate chips

TO MAKE THE BITTEN COOKIE POPS
Line a baking sheet with baking parchment. Using an ice cream scoop, scoop about 2 tablespoons Chocolate Cake Pop Base. Roll into a ball, flatten, and push through a 2-inch (5-cm) round cookie cutter. Place on the prepared baking pan. Using a round crinkle-cutter, cut out a segment on the edge of the cookie to create a bite mark. Repeat the process with the remaining cake pop base. Cover the shapes with plastic wrap and refrigerate for 30 minutes.

Top Pop Tip
Use a teaspoon to pour the candy melt over the pop (over a bowl) if you are finding it difficult to dip the pop into the melted candy coating.

Step One
Melt the candy coating wafers in a bowl over simmering water or in the microwave on the defrost setting. Remove from the heat and let cool for 5 minutes. Meanwhile, remove the cake pops from the refrigerator and let rest for 5 minutes. Dip each lollipop stick about 1 inch (2.5 cm) deep in the melted candy coating, then insert it in the bottom of each cake pop. Place each cake pop, stick up, on the baking pan. Set aside for 15 minutes at room temperature. Keep the candy coating warm.

Step Two
With a knife, cut off the pointed bits on the chocolate chips and discard. Put the chocolate chips to one side. Once the candy coating has secured the lollipop sticks in the pops, dip and swirl each cake pop in the warm candy coating. While the coating is still wet, press on the chocolate chips with the flat sides facing outward.

Step Three
Insert each lollipop stick in a Styrofoam block. Set aside in a cool place, not the refrigerator, for about 30 minutes while the coating sets. Will keep for up to 3 days at room temperature or 1 week in an airtight container in the refrigerator.

Index

Credits

Thanks to the following individuals and suppliers for kindly supplying materials and equipment for pop-making:

Classikool
Classikool cake stands & all things Cake
www.classikool.com
info@classikool.com
www.facebook.com/classikool.ltd
(0044) 1267 281711

Craft Company
graham@craftcompany.co.uk
http://www.craftcompany.co.uk/
info@craftcompany.co.uk

Knightsbridge PME
Paula MacLeod
Deputy Head of Cake Decorating School
Knightsbridge PME Ltd
23 Riverwalk Road
Enfield
EN3 7QN
(0044) 20 3234 0049
(0044) 20 3234 0085
p.macleod@kpme.co.uk
www.knightsbridgepme.co.uk

Planet Bake
Steph Hammond
http://www.planetbake.co.uk/
info@planetbake.co.uk
(0044) 7855073262

Squires Kitchen
Everything you need to make and decorate amazing cakes and fabulous food.

Squires Kitchen
www.squires-shop.com
(0044) 845 61 71 810
customer@squires-shop.com

Sweet Success Sugarcraft and Bakery
rebecca@sweetsuccess.uk.com
info@sweetsuccess.uk.com
www.sweetsuccess.uk.com
(0044) 115 8450660
(0044) 115 8450661

For more information about Tamsin Aston and her company **Definitely Cake**, visit her website: www.DefinitelyCake.com.

With special thanks to Gareth Thomas and my parents for their help and support while writing this book.